Heart Matters

THE PSYCHOLOGY *Of* LOVE & RELATIONSHIP

JOHN M KENNEDY

BlueRose ONE.com
Stories Matter
NewDelhi • London

BLUEROSE PUBLISHERS
India | U.K.

For permissions requests or inquiries regarding this publication,
please contact:

BLUEROSE PUBLISHERS
www.BlueRoseONE.com
info@bluerosepublishers.com
+91 8882 898 898
+4407342408967

ISBN: 978-93-7542-868-8

Cover design: Aafiya Saifi
Typesetting: Manisha Rawat

First Edition: March 2026

Dedication

This Book Is Lovingly Dedicated to The Countless Young Minds Who Seek a Deeper and More Truthful Understanding of The Reality of Love.

Preface

Love is one of the most powerful forces shaping human life, yet it is also among the most misunderstood. It inspires poetry and devotion, joy and sacrifice—but it can equally bring confusion, conflict, and pain. *Heart Matters: The Psychology of Love and Relationship* was written from a simple but profound conviction: when we understand love psychologically, we learn not only how to love others better, but also how to grow as emotionally healthy human beings.

This book is designed as a guided journey through the many dimensions of love and relationships. Drawing from psychological theories, developmental perspectives, and everyday human experiences, it seeks to bridge scientific understanding with real-life emotional realities. The structure of the book reflects the natural progression of human relationships—from attraction, to love, to maturity, and finally to the challenges and healing that often accompany deep emotional bonds.

This book is intended for students, educators, counsellors, and anyone seeking deeper insight into the psychology of love and relationships. It does not promise perfect relationships, but it offers understanding—and understanding is often the first step toward healthier, more meaningful connections.

If this book encourages readers to reflect more honestly on their emotions, relate more compassionately with others, and approach love with maturity and responsibility, then it will have fulfilled its purpose.

John M Kennedy

04 February 2026

Rev. Dr. Darline Joseph Marianathan
UKCP 2011171976, BACP 00952039 & BPS 406325
Doctoral Psychotherapist (completed) & Psychologist (final year)
(DCPsych- Metanoia/Middlesex University, England)
MEd Psychology BPS (Bristol University, England)
MSC Psychology (Exeter University, England)
MSC Psychology, BA Economics, BTh &BPh (India)

Foreword

Anyone who opens this book on *love* will undoubtedly find themselves falling in love with it. Fr. Kennedy has invested years of thoughtful and thorough research into this subject, presenting his insights in a manner that is both scholarly and wonderfully accessible. Readers from every walk of life will find it engaging, enriching, and deeply beneficial.

As a psychologist with a background in neuroscience, I can affirm the author's skilful integration of theoretical depth and practical wisdom. His attention to the finer nuances of love and human relationships is evident throughout, offering clarity without oversimplification.

I am confident that readers will be attracted to this book from the very first chapter, *The Psychology of Attraction*. The book's unique style of presentation, combined with its wide-ranging themes within the single subject of love, makes it both refreshing and compelling.

Fr. Kennedy's exploration of love across different relationships between parents and children, between boys and girls, and between partners; is expressed with simplicity, insight, and remarkable beauty.

I wholeheartedly recommend this book to everyone: fathers and mothers, brothers and sisters, boys and girls, lovers and partners, and people of every faith tradition; Christians, Hindus, Muslims, as well as those who follow no religion. Do not miss this book. It will be a treasured addition to your bookshelf.

I warmly congratulate Fr. Kennedy for his painstaking and dedicated effort in producing this outstanding work for the good of society. I wish him every blessing and continued inspiration for many more such books in the years to come.

With Regards
Rev. Dr. Darline Joseph Marianathan
07 January 2026
London

Registered Member **399801**
MBACP

Contents

Introduction

"Words are like battles", a famous general once said "the right word is the battle won, an inaccurate word is a defeat." The word "Love" is a defeat, because in the contemporary society, love is widely used and frequently misunderstood. It fills magazines and headlines, celebrated for its power and blamed for the crimes and tragedies it inspires. Popular media, social networks, films, and literature often portray love in exaggerated or unrealistic ways, reducing a complex psychological experience to a simple emotion or fantasy. As a result, the concept of love has become blurred, despite its profound influence on human behaviour and mental health. Men have killed for love, women have died for it, and countless lives have been shaped by its presence or absence. Hence, Love remains one of the most frequently discussed yet least clearly defined human experiences.

Helen Keller beautifully expressed this when she said, "The best and most beautiful things in the world cannot be seen or touched. They must be felt with the heart." Love belongs to this invisible world of feelings. Everyone understands love differently, based on personal experiences, emotions, and expectations. This is why there are countless definitions of love, yet no single definition that feels complete. Love may be impossible to fully define, but it deeply influences how we think, feel, and relate to others. A youngster who feels excited waiting for a message, anxious about a reply, or heartbroken after being ignored is already learning about love—often without realizing it. This book attempts to understand love from a psychological point of view—going beyond fantasy and emotion to explore how love actually works.

Victor Hugo the renowned French poet and author, wrote, "The greatest happiness of life is the conviction that we are loved." The need to love and to be loved is a fundamental human motivation - it spans all stages of life, from young adulthood, when individuals search for intimacy and companionship, to later years, when emotional connection continues to provide meaning and comfort. For young people, this feeling can be deeply intense. A simple smile, a compliment, or feeling "chosen" by someone special can boost confidence and self-worth. At the same time, rejection or emotional neglect can feel devastating. This shows that love is not just an emotion—it affects identity, self-esteem, and mental health. However, the desire to love is not love itself. Love is revealed through action. It is an act of will—an intentional choice followed by responsible behaviour.

Love is neither accidental nor static; it is not a fixed state between two unchanging individuals. Rather, it is a psychological and emotional journey that often begins with the ecstasy of attraction, passes through self-discovery and challenges, and, at its best, culminates in an intimate, joyful, lifelong union.

Love and relationships occupy a central place in the emotional lives of young people. Adolescence and early adulthood are marked by intense emotions, curiosity, vulnerability, and a longing for meaningful connection. During these formative years, attraction can be powerful, relationships deeply influential, and experiences of love—whether fulfilling or painful—can leave lasting psychological impressions. Yet, despite its importance, love is frequently misunderstood, idealized, or approached without adequate emotional or psychological insight. This book seeks to explore love not as a romantic fantasy or fleeting emotion, but as a complex psychological process shaped by biology, personality, upbringing, social influences, and emotional maturity.

Human beings are inherently relational. Relationships play a vital role in shaping identity, self-esteem, emotional regulation, and overall well-being. For young people especially, love and attraction often serve as pathways to self-discovery, while also becoming sources of confusion, anxiety, conflict, and emotional pain. For instance, a child who grew up feeling emotionally supported may find it easier to trust in relationships. Another who experienced neglect or criticism may struggle with self-doubt, jealousy, or fear of rejection. Understanding these patterns helps youngsters realize that their relationship struggles are not personal failures, but psychological patterns that can be understood and changed.

This book begins by examining attraction and interpersonal relationships, exploring why people are drawn to one another and how psychological, social, and emotional factors influence attraction. Various theories are discussed to provide scientific explanations for how relationships form and develop. Attraction, as this book reveals, is not accidental but follows identifiable psychological patterns that shape how relationships begin and evolve.

This book delves into the meaning and nature of love as a multidimensional experience. It examines emotional maturity, parental love, self-love, friendship, and romantic love, emphasizing how early family relationships and childhood experiences influence later patterns of intimacy. For example, someone who lacks self-love may tolerate disrespect just to avoid being alone. Learning to value oneself is a foundation for healthy relationships. Further, the theories of falling in love, hormonal influences, and gender expectations are discussed to clarify why love often feels intense, transformative, and at times overwhelming—particularly during youth.

Love, however, is not free from struggle. Issues such as the relationship between love and sexuality, premarital intimacy, jealousy, possessiveness, emotional dependency, self-doubt, unrealistic expectations, communication barriers, childhood wounds, and heartbreak are examined with psychological sensitivity. Rather than portraying love as purely blissful or tragically painful, this book presents love as a dynamic process that requires awareness, communication, responsibility, and emotional growth. It also offers guidance on healing after heartbreak—understanding that pain does not mean failure, but an opportunity for self-discovery and growth.

Ultimately, this book aims to help young readers move beyond fantasy and fear toward a deeper, more mature understanding of love. It presents love as a powerful force capable of nurturing personal growth, deepening self-knowledge, and enriching life when approached with psychological insight, emotional balance, and respect for oneself and others. By integrating theory, reflection, and real-life relevance, the book seeks to guide readers toward healthier relationships and a more meaningful experience of love. Its purpose is to plunge into the ocean of human experience and surface the buried treasure called love—offering clarity, understanding, and guidance to those who seek it.

What You'll Gain from This Book

After reading this book, you will be able to:

- **Understand the concept of love from a psychological perspective**

  Explain how love differs from attraction, infatuation, and emotional dependency.

- **Recognize the role of love in human development and mental health**

  Describe how love and relationships influence self-esteem, identity formation, emotional regulation, and well-being, especially during adolescence and early adulthood.

- **Explain psychological theories related to attraction and relationships**

  Identify key psychological, social, and biological factors that contribute to attraction and relationship formation.

- **Differentiate between healthy and unhealthy relationship patterns**

  Analyze behaviors such as respect, communication, control, jealousy, and emotional dependence using psychological concepts.

- **Understand the developmental nature of love**

  Describe how love evolves over time through stages such as attraction, bonding, conflict, adjustment, and growth.

- **Examine the influence of early relationships on later love experiences**

  Explain how childhood attachment and family relationships shape adult romantic patterns.

- **Identify common emotional challenges in love and relationships**
  Discuss issues such as jealousy, insecurity, unrealistic expectations, heartbreak, and emotional pain from a psychological viewpoint.
- **Apply psychological insights to real-life situations**
  Use psychological concepts to interpret everyday relationship experiences among young people.
- **Develop emotional awareness and relational responsibility**
  Reflect on the importance of self-love, emotional maturity, and personal responsibility in forming healthy relationships.
- **Cultivate a realistic and mature understanding of love**
  Move beyond idealized or media-driven views of love toward an informed, balanced psychological understanding.

Part One
Interpersonal Attraction And Relationship

Human life is inherently social, and the quality of our interactions significantly influences our overall well-being. Interpersonal attraction and relationships form the foundation of human experience, shaping how connections begin, develop, and endure over time. Attraction is not a single or accidental process; rather, it emerges from the interaction of biological, psychological, social, and cultural factors. Understanding these influences helps explain why certain relationships grow stronger while others fade. Across friendships, romantic partnerships, family relationships, and professional settings, interpersonal attraction and relationships reflect essential aspects of human motivation, identity, and social functioning. The first part of this book examines key theoretical perspectives and research findings on interpersonal attraction and relationships, highlighting their importance in human life.

1
Psychology of Attraction

Human beings are inherently social creatures. Therefore, it is natural for each individual to feel attraction towards others. This attraction carries psychological significances. The psychology of attraction explores why we are drawn to certain people and not to others. It examines how biological instincts, emotions, and cognitive processes influence attraction. Physical appearance, similarity, and proximity play important roles in initial attraction. Psychological factors such as personality, values, and attachment styles shape deeper connections. Social and cultural norms also guide whom we find attractive and acceptable as partners. Hence, understanding the key factors that contribute to attraction and examining how they ultimately manifest in romantic relationships is essential.

Interpersonal Attraction

In the nineteenth century, poet Elizabeth Barrett Browning wrote, "How do I love thee? Let me count the ways," expressing deep emotions about love. This idea reflects a topic that is central to many people's lives and has since become an important area of study for social psychologists. Today, this field is known as interpersonal attraction, which focuses on loving and liking.

Interpersonal Attraction is crucial in all types of relationships, particularly in the context of Lovemaking. It refers to the assessment of others based on how much we like or dislike them. It can also be described as the positive feelings we have towards others, encompassing both liking and loving. Research in attraction aims to identify the specific factors that influence these interpersonal evaluations. Some social psychologists suggest that we tend to make positive evaluations when our feelings are favourable and negative evaluations when our feelings are unfavourable. Therefore, an individual's likes and dislikes are largely shaped by their emotions. Any element that impacts emotions will also influence attraction, regardless of the source of those emotions. In essence, interpersonal attraction pertains to the judgment one person forms about another.

The Factors of Attraction

What draws people to one another initially? What processes contribute to the evolution of relationships as they progress? The answers lie in the various factors identified by social psychologists that play a crucial role in the formation and sustenance of interpersonal attractions and relationships. These factors serve as the foundational and initial aspects of Loving and Liking.

1. **Proximity**

   Proximity refers to closeness (deriving from the same root as approximate). It is described as "a factor that has been demonstrated to influence the level of attraction one individual feels towards another." In simpler terms, being near to someone is a reason for liking them. Consequently, physical proximity serves as the initial step in fostering attraction between individuals. This explains why people are more inclined to form friendships or romantic relationships with those who are geographically close, whether in living or working situations. Being close to someone enhances the chances of getting to know them better. Thus, Proximity facilitates familiarity.

   - **Mere Exposure Effect**

     It arises from proximity. It suggests that "Repeated exposure to a person is often enough to generate attraction." Attraction often develops when individuals have repeated interactions with certain people more frequently than with others. In essence, repeated exposure to any stimulus fosters attraction. If the initial experience with that stimulus is positive, it results in 'liking'; conversely, if it is negative, it leads to 'disliking.' Zajonc (1968) posited in his theory that, "With repeated exposure to any mild negative, neutral, or positive stimulus, the assessment of that stimulus becomes progressively more favourable."

It is a straightforward yet accurate observation that individuals often experience at least mild discomfort when encountering anything or anyone unfamiliar. Over time, with continued exposure, feelings of anxiety diminish, and the new entity or individual gradually becomes more familiar. Typically, this repeated exposure is influenced by one's physical environment or residential closeness or proximity.

- **Familiarity**

  Proximity contributes to familiarity, which results from repeated exposure to an individual. Research indicates that familiarity, rather than fostering contempt, typically enhances affection for others (Moreland & Zajonc, 1982).

  In a study conducted in 1968, Zajonc presented participants with photographs of various individuals. Some images were displayed frequently, while others were shown less often. Subsequently, participants were asked to evaluate their feelings towards the individuals depicted in the photographs. Those whose images were frequently viewed were rated as more likable compared to those whose images were seen only once or twice. This demonstrates that, in real-life scenarios, individuals tend to like or love most those with whom they share the greatest familiarity.

2. Attitude Similarity

Psychologists assert that shared backgrounds, interests, values, and attitudes enhance the strength of interpersonal attraction between individuals. Folk wisdom tells that, "*Birds of a feather flock together*." Therefore, attitude similarity refers to the inclination to favour those who resemble us. In other words, if two individuals begin to interact, their feelings of liking or disliking are heavily influenced by their similarities in attitudes, beliefs, values, and other traits. Whether it involves physical traits like height, age, and attractiveness, or psychological traits such as attitudes and personalities, people generally prefer those who are similar to them over those who are not. To put it differently, the degree to which two individuals share similar attitudes on various topics tends to attract them to each other.

The survey studies conducted by Laumann (1969) and Towhey (1972) have substantiated the aforementioned statements. The underlying reason for the inclination to feel attraction towards similar individuals lies in the belief that people with comparable attitudes will evaluate others favourably.

To demonstrate that similar attitudes were the cause of attraction, Theodore M. Newcomb elucidated this concept through his "Balance theory." However, Rosenbaum (1986) challenged this notion in his "Repulsion hypothesis," asserting that "Attraction is not amplified by similar attitudes; rather, individuals initially react positively to others but become repulsed upon discovering differing attitudes." In this context, he merely suggested that dissimilar attitudes diminish attraction, while similar attitudes exert no influence.

- **The Matching Hypothesis**

  The matching hypothesis posits that individuals are drawn to one another as friends, romantic partners, or spouses based on shared characteristics such as physical attractiveness, age, race, personality traits, or social resources like wealth, education, or power. It can be summarized as "Liking others who are similar to yourself." In 1870, Sir Francis Galton was the first to articulate this concept as "Like marries like."

  Research indicates that couples with dissimilar attributes tend to experience less satisfying relationships compared to those who share similar levels of attractiveness and characteristics (Forgas, 1993). The principle of matching for attractiveness is also evident in same-sex friendships among both men and women; overall, friendly and romantic relationships frequently stem from the recognition of attitude similarity.

3. **Physical Attractiveness**

Physical attractiveness serves as a primary factor in determining attraction. Despite cultural sayings like "Beauty is only skin deep" and "you can't judge a book by its cover," individuals tend to respond strongly to physical appeal. Physical attractiveness refers to a combination of facial and bodily features that are perceived as aesthetically pleasing (for instance, beautiful or handsome) by others. For many, the association of beauty with goodness is quite significant, leading to the conclusion that a physically attractive person is generally more popular than someone who is not, even when all other factors are equal. This holds particularly true in romantic contexts.

In fact, these preferences manifest quite early in life. For instance, a study involving infants aged six to eight months revealed that when shown two photographs of different women—one deemed attractive by adults and the other unattractive—the infants spent a significantly longer time gazing at the attractive face compared to the unattractive one (Langlois et al, 1987). This explains why attractive women often secure their positions based on their appearance rather than their competencies. In 1972, two American researchers found that this principle even influences how teachers interact with their students. Evidence suggests that the academic grades assigned to students are affected by the child's attractiveness.

- **Physical Attractiveness and Positive Affect**

  A crucial factor in attraction is affect. Individuals who are good-looking evoke positive feelings: Men and women exhibit some differences; specifically, men are more influenced by female attractiveness than women are by male attractiveness. Evolutionary theory posits that attractiveness signals good health.

  Singh (1993) notes that men particularly respond to a woman's waist-to-hip ratio. Men tend to prefer women with smaller waists and consider them attractive, healthy, and reproductively valuable. Clearly, attractiveness is not necessarily linked to health or fertility. Cunning's research (1986) indicates that the most attractive women possess either 'childlike' features, such as large, widely spaced eyes and a small nose and chin, or 'mature' features, including prominent cheekbones, narrow cheeks, high eyebrows, large pupils, and a broad smile.

In summary, people tend to expect to like attractive individuals, treat them more favourably, and as a result, attractive people become more likable. When attraction evolves into a deeper, inner connection, love begins to flourish.

- **Appearance Anxiety**

  People often worry about their appearance because they fear being judged negatively by others and are concerned about how attractive they seem. This worry is called appearance anxiety.

  It is defined as "Apprehension or worry about the adequacy of one's physical appearance and how it is perceived by others." Research indicates that women experience higher levels of appearance anxiety compared to men, which can result in discomfort during social interactions.

4. Need Complementarity Hypothesis

Need Complementarity Hypothesis suggests that "People are attracted to others who fulfil their needs." It posits that people are most satisfied in relationships when their needs are complementary rather than similar. In other words, People seek out relationships where their own characteristics or needs are complemented - not necessarily mirrored - by their partners. This hypothesis stands in contrast to the concept of attitude similarity.

According to this perspective, a person may find themselves attracted to those who fulfil or complement the most needs for them. In other words, this hypothesis argues that people are attracted to others whose traits or needs compliment (or contrast with) their own. For instance, a dominant individual might seek a submissive partner, while a submissive person may look for someone dominant.

This hypothesis was popularised in part through the work of Robert F. Winch in the 1950s and 60s. He argued that need complementarity, rather than similarity, was the key to marital satisfaction. In general, similarity may matter more in the early stages, while complementarity may become more important in maintaining long term satisfaction.

5. **Confirmation of Self-Esteem**

   People may receive both positive and negative evaluations from others. In these situations, they usually choose to like or love those who support and confirm their view of themselves. People with very low self-esteem often prefer being around others who also see them negatively, because it feels familiar or comfortable. However, this tendency can lead to harmful consequences

   Specifically, an individual with a low self-evaluation may select friends, romantic partners, and even spouses who consistently criticize them. The cumulative effect of such criticism can further diminish their self-esteem. The awareness that someone else perceives them as a worthy individual offers a sense of security ("a reward") and contributes to their overall well-being.

6. **Reciprocity: Mutual Affection**

   Individuals tend to favour those who express positive feelings towards them and assess them more favourably than those who do not. There is also some indication that a person is more likely to be drawn to others who demonstrate their affection in some manner. Thus, the tendency to return compliments or expressed feelings of interest or affection is referred to as reciprocity.

1. The Equity Principle

As per the exchange or equity principle, "Social relationships are transactions in which partners exchange goods and services." In certain romantic relationships, the transactional aspect can be quite evident. For instance, in the matrimonial section of a newspaper or website candidates outline their qualifications and other attributes, while also specifying certain qualities they seek in return. Similar to business transactions, if both partners perceive the arrangement as equitable, then the friendship or romantic relationship is likely to be more stable. When both partners are equally attractive and intelligent, and contribute similarly to financial aspects, establishing a fair deal becomes easy.

However, there are instances where one partner may be wealthier while the other is more attractive, or one may possess greater intelligence while the other is exceptionally kind and considerate, or some other form of compensation may exist. Although these arrangements may appear fair, ensuring their longevity can be more challenging. In other words, such relationships may not endure over time.

2
Psychology of Relationship

The studies of attraction have primarily focused on brief encounters between unfamiliar individuals. Furthermore, these studies have provided insights into the factors that influence initial attraction, which in turn shape the nature of a relationship as it evolves over time. Without relationships, an individual cannot truly understand others or develop their own identity. Relationships not only facilitate self-discovery; but also contribute to personal growth. Through interactions with others, one learns the essence of love. C.G. Jung once remarked, "One is always in the dark about one's own personality; one needs others to get to know oneself."

In this context, the term 'relationship' implies intimacy, and it is within the family unit that individuals first acquire the fundamental aspects of love, affection, tenderness, and loyalty. The nature of each person's interpersonal relationship is established in the interaction between an infant and the primary caregiver—typically the mother.

The Evolution of a Relationship

The social exchange theorists have established a framework to elucidate the nature and dynamics of interpersonal relationships. According to J.P. Chaplin, "Interpersonal relationship is that which occurs between persons or characterizing process that arises as a result of the interaction of individuals." Michael Argyle asserts that there are seven fundamental drives aimed at various objectives that motivate individuals to cultivate relationships with others, they are: non-social drives (to fulfil biological or financial needs), dependency, dominance, the need for affiliation, sex, aggression, and self-esteem.

i. **Stimulus - Values - Role (SVR) Theory**

In this theory, psychologist Bernard Murstein proposed a sequential order of three stages through which relationships develop. These stages are as follows:

- *The Stimulus Stage:* At this stage, relationships are formed based on superficial, physical traits, such as a person's appearance. Typically, this represents only the initial meeting.
- *The Value Stage:* This stage generally occurs between the second and seventh meetings, where the relationship is defined by increasing similarity of values and beliefs.
- *The Role Stage:* In this stage, the relationship is defined by specific roles (such as boyfriend-girlfriend or husband-wife) assumed by the individuals involved.

While stimulus, value, and role factors are predominant at certain stages, they also play a role at other points in the evolving relationship. Not all relationships follow this exact pattern, which has led to some criticism of the SVR theory.

ii. **Social Exchange Theory**

The social exchange theory, introduced by John Thibaut and Harold Kelley, serves as a framework for understanding social relationships. This theory highlights the interdependence inherent in all relationships. It functions as an economic system where individuals involved in a relationship rely on one another for the quality of outcomes they derive from that relationship; it encompasses comparison levels and alternative comparison levels. According to this theory, the quality of outcomes is influenced by the behaviours of both participants engaged in the relationship.

This theory is also valuable for understanding the evolving nature of relationships as they progress from initial contact to a deeper level of intimacy. In this context, George Levinger and J. Diedrick Snock have identified three primary levels of involvement in relationship development.

1. **Unilateral Awareness:** This is the most superficial level, where an individual evaluates the characteristics of another person and forms judgments about them. At this stage, they assess whether the relationship will be beneficial in the future.

2. **Surface Contact:** This level occurs when two individuals begin to interact. A key function of this stage is self-disclosure, defined as "the process through which one person allows another to know them better," which involves sharing thoughts, feelings, and past experiences. The decisions made during self-disclosure significantly influence the potential development of the relationship.

3. **Stage of Mutuality:** If partners find their interactions at the surface contact level rewarding and promising, the relationship may advance to the stage of mutuality. At this stage, each individual starts to feel a sense of responsibility for the relationship's outcomes, which their partner experiences. Consequently, both individuals act in ways that enhance their own outcomes as well as those of their partner.

Level of Relationship	Development
0. Zero contact (two unrelated persons)	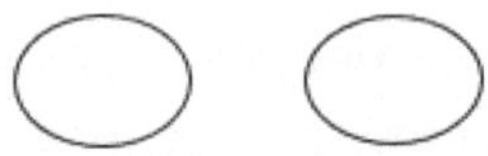
1. Awareness (Unilateral or impressions; no interactions)	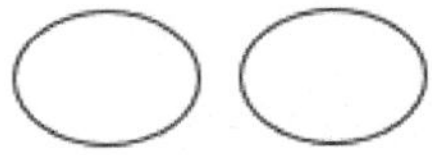
2. Surface contact (Bilateral attitudes; Some interaction)	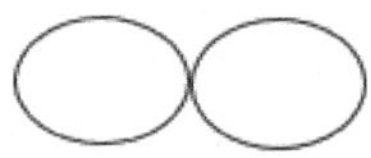
3. Mutuality (a continuum) 3.1. Minor intersection E.g., workplace relationship	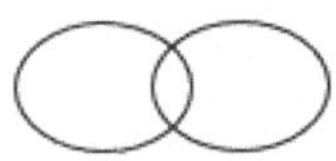
3.2 Major intersection E.g., Friendship	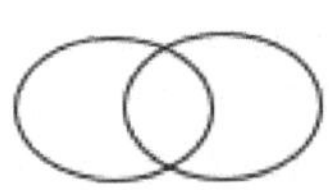
3.3 Total Unity (The fantastic extreme) E.g., Love and marriage unity	

- As a relationship matures, it progresses through different phases. (Adapted from Levinger & Snock, 1972)

The Significance of Interpersonal Relationships

a) Interpersonal relationships are essential for human existence. Interacting with others contributes to self-awareness, shaping one's attitudes, values, and concepts through their behaviour with others.

b) Through this interaction, a person gains a comprehensive understanding of themselves, which facilitates behavioural changes and enhances interpersonal effectiveness.

c) It provides insight into others' motivations during social interactions, fostering mutual exchanges and affection.

d) Establishing friendships and partnerships, particularly in marriage and other areas of life, is crucial. It emphasizes the importance of communication with others, including problem-solving and presenting oneself positively.

e) It enables individuals to share their innermost selves with trusted friends and enjoy meaningful experiences together, such as interpersonal fun, pleasure, and self-gratification.

Beyond our shared humanity, each individual and relationship is distinct. Nevertheless, in a healthy relationship the convergence of two energy systems sparks a dynamic exchange that enables each person to flourish and become a more complete version of themselves.

One clear takeaway from the key determinants of relationships is that attraction cannot flourish unless both individuals are eager to form a connection and respond positively to each other's observable traits. Therefore, in any relationship, particularly in romantic contexts, the characteristics of the individuals play a crucial role in transforming attraction into a meaningful relationship. The following pages will discuss the elements of attraction and the progression of love relationships between two individuals, as well as the essence and characteristics of love.

Part Two
The Phenomenon of Love

Love is one of the most powerful yet complex experiences in human life. It is expressed as a deep sense of care and affection in which concern for another may equal or even exceed concern for oneself. Although its origins cannot be clearly defined, love appears fundamental to life and human development, beginning with early bonds such as those between parent and child and extending to relationships, ideals, and values throughout life. Being loved and understood is essential for personal growth, a meaningful life, and a sense of self-worth, as the absence of love often leads to feelings of emptiness. At the same time, love can become harmful when it is not expressed in healthy ways. Therefore, understanding love from different perspectives is crucial for recognizing its role in shaping human growth and well-being. The second part of this book examines various perspectives on love, the different terms used to describe it, and its role in the process of human development.

1
The Various Perspective on Love

A man naturally reveals love to his fellow beings. Love is an inherent quality that is consistently displayed in humans and it gradually develops over time. In contemporary society, the meaning of love has been shaped by the highly charged erotic environment of the modern world. To understand its meaning solely based on these factors is to overlook the complete picture. Love can be characterized as a profound feeling of deep affection for someone or something, particularly for a family member or a friend.

Love cannot be treated as a tangible substance that can be separated and examined. The more one delves into the concept of 'love,' the more elusive it becomes. The very fact that, after millennia of human existence, individuals continue to inquire 'what is Love?' suggests that the question lacks a definitive answer. It appears that Love is what one chooses to make of it. Each individual appears to have their own interpretation of love; however, there seems to be a unanimity on several aspects of love, which will be elaborated upon in the following pages.

A General Perspective on Love

Love, in a broader sense, is a fundamental force that tends to unite two individuals. It can exist as one-sided or mutual, but a reciprocal love is essential to achieve the union. Fundamentally, love is about respecting another person as an individual. Love cannot exist without respect, just as lungs cannot function without air. Love is never merely the selfishness of two individuals or a desire to dominate the other.

Love promises growth, maturity, and happiness in one's life. Saint Exupery states, "Love does not consist in gazing at each other, but in looking outward together in the same direction." Bernard R. Young Man expresses, "Love is the strong feeling of 'being together' that reveals our true selves."

For some individuals, love is merely an emotional reaction. It begins and concludes with the physical aspect. It represents a rational, even fervent attraction towards another, which essentially equates to sexual desire. Conversely, for others, love signifies a readiness to make sacrifices. Undoubtedly, both perspectives can guide one towards a deeper comprehension of love; however, in isolation, they do not constitute love.

Gerald Vann O.P states, "Love is not something that is handed over, pre-fabricated, but rather something that must be cultivated with considerable effort, dedication, and struggle." Love cannot be acquired at a bargain, and those who attempt to do so are often the first to experience pain. Love does not always seek to bargain for itself; it simply desires to bless the other.

Love is famously blind: once ignited, it overcomes all barriers to achieve its objective. It disregards the cost. In essence, love represents a unique connection with another. It establishes a bond between two individuals while they continue to exist as separate entities, united in love. To love means to care about others. It involves truly listening, understanding their feelings, and seeing things from their point of view instead of judging them. Loving someone also means giving your time and abilities and emotionally connecting with them, especially when they are struggling.

Psychological Perspective on Love

According to S.T. Coleridge, "love is a desire of the whole being felt to be united to something or some being is necessary to its completeness, by the most perfect means that nature permits and reason dictates." Love is not about reaching out to take, but rather about giving. It does not focus on oneself, but rather shows concern for another, wishing for that person's goodness and happiness.

Dr. Harry Stack Sullivan, in his conceptions of modern psychiatry states, "When the satisfaction, security, and development of another person become as significant to one as his own satisfaction, security, and development, love exists."

Erich Fromm asserts: Love is an activity, not a passive effect; it is a "standing in" rather than a "falling for." He further explains, "It is an illusion to claim that there should not be struggle and crisis in love, for love is a challenge, not a resting place. Whether the lovers are in communion or in conflict, their love continuously moves and grows without any stagnation."

Philosophical Perspective on Love

Empedocles, a member of the metaphysical pluralist school, asserted that love and hate serve as the fundamental forces responsible for the emergence of all things. For him, love represents the governing principle of the universe, fostering unity, order, goodness, and growth within it.

In Indian philosophy, love is seen as the main force behind the creation of the universe. At first, the cosmos existed in a quiet, formless state, filled with Brahman, or cosmic consciousness. When Brahman became self-aware and experienced self-love, it formed the thought, "I am one; let me become many." This thought led to the creation of the universe. In this way, love is believed to be the divine source of all creation.

Emmanuel Levinas posits that "the love relationship is one in which the lover's desire extends beyond merely loving the other (the beloved) to also wishing for the beloved to reciprocate that love." Thomas Aquinas states, "To love anyone is nothing other than to wish for that person's well-being." The existentialist philosopher Gabriel Marcel contends that 'availability' is the essence of love. He asserts, "One must be free (available) to transcend one's own self and selfish concerns, reaching out to others with a complete readiness to listen. In this context, the beloved becomes the focal point of one's world and the centre of one's attention."

Another existentialist philosopher Martin Buber explains that feelings exist within a person, but love is something a person lives in. Love is not just a feeling directed at someone as an object. Instead, it exists in the relationship between "I and Thou," meaning a genuine, mutual connection between two people. According to Buber, love involves responsibility and care of one person ("I") for another ("Thou").

Spiritual Perspective on Love

Thomas Aquinas says that we describe God using analogies because God is a mystery and cannot be fully understood or expressed in human language. Nonetheless, one term provides the fundamental connection to God's nature and actions, which is 'Love'. The creation, its sustenance, and redemption can all be understood in terms of love. The Bible states, "God is Love, and anyone who lives in love lives in God, and God lives in him" (1John 4:16).

Love is undoubtedly a divine quality of the human mind. It is the purest reflection of God. Indeed, it represents God residing in the hearts of men. Thus, Love serves as a window into the very essence of God. If one comprehends love in its entirety, he would grasp all there is to know about God himself. Love is the sacred altar at which human relationships—spiritual, mental, or physical—are sanctified. The act of love itself is grace, as one can only love God through God's strength and power, since human love is merely a response to His love.

In God, there exists no hunger that requires fulfilment; rather, there is an abundance that yearns to give. God would not keep His goodness, and the act of sharing it resulted in creation. Thus, there is a fundamental connection between divine and human love in the context of agape. The creative nature of divine love seeks to manifest in the gracious love of human beings towards their God and fellow humans.

A person who tries to live by God's love returns that love back to God. Since God desires nothing for Himself, how can one reciprocate God's love? This is achieved by recognizing God in others. A genuine love for creation is inherently religious: "I love you as God intends you to be." Conversely, a false love for creation is sacrilegious: "I refuse to accept you as you were originally created."

God's love did not conclude with creation; it continuously fosters humanity. All individuals are the complete and total focus of God's attentive love. If God were to cease loving, even for a moment, humanity would cease to exist, disintegrating and returning to nothingness. It is through God's love that a person achieves his goal of securing eternal happiness. The wonder of wonders is that God has willingly chosen to share this divine gift of love with humanity, placing them at the heart of His existence, dedicating all His divine energies to their well-being and happiness. To address issues of sexual inconsistency and conflict, humanity relies solely on spiritual love, as it allows one to view the beloved as a divine gift.

2
The Terms for Love

The English language encompasses a single term for the concept of love, which is employed in numerous contexts to convey a variety of emotions, resulting in a lack of a precise definition. As a result, its meaning is predominantly shaped by the context in which it is used. For instance, "I love Switzerland in the summer," "I love cotton Shirts," "I love Angelina", as all these phrases utilize the term 'Love' interchangeably.

In contrast, the ancient Greeks had a rich understanding of love and distinguished between different kinds of love rather than seeing it as a single, universal emotion. They used specific terms to capture the nuances of different relationships and emotional bonds. Here are the seven main types of love identified by the Greeks.

1. Eros – Romantic, Passionate Love

Nature: Intense, sexual, and passionate desire.

Characteristics: Often irrational, all-consuming, and driven by physical attraction.

Source: Named after the Greek god of love and fertility.

Modern Equivalent: Romantic or sexual love.

Note: Eros can be overwhelming and was sometimes seen as dangerous or a loss of control.

Eros represents the physical and sexual aspect of love. It embodies the need, desire, and longing for another person on a physical level. Eros is perceived as sex-love, which encompasses biological, glandular, instinctual, and emotional elements. The Romans referred to Eros as Cupid, who pierces the hearts of humans with the arrow of love.

Eros often fails to differentiate between pleasure and the individual. In Eros, it is the pleasure derived from the other person that is truly cherished. This form of erotic love can sometimes transform into hatred. However, this transformation is unlikely if genuine love exists, as love would persist regardless of whether the other person reciprocates. By its very nature, erotic love represents a rather immature form of affection.

2. Philia - Deep Friendship or Affectionate Love

Nature: Platonic, loyal, and virtuous love.

Characteristics: Based on mutual respect, shared experiences, and goodwill.

Context: Common in close friendships, comrades-in-arms, or intellectual partnerships.

Modern Equivalent: Deep friendship or brotherly love.

The term 'Philia' is the origin of the English word 'filial'. Its fundamental meaning pertains to brotherly love. However, in Greek, 'brotherly' is not confined to kinship and can also describe an attitude and quality of connection where the care felt between blood relatives is similarly experienced between those who are not related by blood.

Philia embodies the love found in friendship and brotherhood, and it can also manifest within marriage. This type of love is founded on a shared sense of feeling, interest, or service; it is the intellect, rather than physical desires, that guides the affections. In erotic love, the other person can be substituted; in Philia, the beloved is irreplaceable, as no one can take the place of a close friend, a devoted spouse, or a cherished mother.

3. Storge - Familial Love

Nature: Natural affection, especially between parents and children.

Characteristics: Often unconditional, built on familiarity and dependency.

Context: Seen in family relationships, but also sometimes used to describe love for one's country or pets.

Modern Equivalent: Parental or familial love.

Storge represents the most instinctive and natural form of love—the kind that arises without effort or conscious intention. It is typically the first kind of love a person experience, often from their parents or caregivers. This love is not chosen but emerges naturally, often through proximity, familiarity, and life-long bonds. For example, a mother instinctively loving and caring for her new-born child, or siblings developing affection over years of growing up together.

Storge doesn't require the loved one to meet certain conditions or standards. A parent still loves their child even when they misbehave or disappoint. It grows over time through shared experiences—living together, going through struggles and joys side by side. It often forms between people who depend on each other—physically, emotionally, or socially. Children depend on parents, but parents can also grow emotionally dependent on their children.

Ancient Greeks and later thinkers sometimes used the term more broadly to include: A person's patriotic love for their homeland and the affection someone has for their pets, which often mirrors parental affection.

4. Agape - Selfless, Unconditional Love

Nature: Altruistic, spiritual, and universal love.

Characteristics: Given without expecting anything in return; compassionate and empathetic.

Context: Associated with divine love (e.g., in Christian theology, God's love for humanity).

Modern Equivalent: Charity, love for all, or unconditional love.

Agape love represents the liberating force that compels one to address a neighbour's needs without anticipating any reward in return. It is a gift given without conditions. It embodies the altruistic, generous, and non-demanding aspects of love. This form of love actively concerns with the life and development of the beloved. It is not dependent upon the worth or value of the other and when it is expressed it carries no obligation - it is an unconditional gift. The dominant trends regard Agape as distinctively Christian love, which originates from God, but is also truly expressed in human love for God and neighbour. Agape is born of divine strength. It has power to wait, to accept life, to find goodness in living, even in sufferings.

5. Ludus - Playful Love

Nature: Light-hearted, flirtatious love.

Characteristics: Without deep commitment; involves teasing, laughter, and fun.

Context: Found in the early stages of romance or casual interactions.

Modern Equivalent: Flirting or infatuation.

Ludus is playful, flirtatious, or casual love often characterised by a sense of fun, excitement, and adventure. In the adolescent stage, it is expressed in the form of infatuation. Ludus involves a carefree and light-hearted approach to relationships, with an emphasis on enjoyment and pleasure. In modern terms Ludus might manifest as; flirting, casual dating, playful teasing, romantic games or challenges, a focus on having fun and enjoy each other's company. Ludus is often associated with the early stages of romance or relationships, where the excitement and thrill of getting to know someone new or paramount. However, it can also be a persistent aspect of a relationship, keeping things fresh and playful.

6. Pragma – Enduring Love

Nature: Practical, long-term love.

Characteristics: Built on commitment, understanding, and mutual goals.

Context: Found in mature relationships, such as long marriages or partnerships.

Modern Equivalent: Long-lasting, realistic love based on reason and compromise.

Pragma is enduring, practical and committed love, often characterised by a deep sense of responsibility, loyalty and dedication. Pragma involves a mature and pragmatic approach to relationships prioritizing long term commitment, building a life together, shared responsibilities and decision making, emotional support and stability, a focus on working through challenges and growing together.

Pragma is often associated with mature established relationships where partners have built a strong foundation of trust, understanding, and cooperation. It is the love that develops overtime through shared experiences, and a deepening commitment to one another. Pragma is not just about feelings, but also about actions, choices, and a willingness to work together to build a life. It is a love that is grounded in reality, and it is often characterised by sense of stability and security and mutual support.

7. Philautia – Self-Love

Nature: Love directed at oneself.

Two Forms:

- **Healthy:** Self-respect and self-compassion.
- **Unhealthy:** Narcissism or arrogance.

Context: The Greeks saw healthy self-love as essential to loving others.

Modern Equivalent: Self-esteem or narcissism, depending on context.

In Greek philosophy, Philautia refers to the love of oneself, which can be healthy (self-respect and self-care) or unhealthy (selfishness or narcissism), depending on how it is expressed. The key aspects of philautia are Self-acceptance, self-care, self-awareness, self-compassion and self-forgiveness. It increases one's self-esteem and confidence and by cultivating philautia one can develop a more positive and compassionate relationship with oneself, leading to greater overall well-being and life satisfaction.

These concepts helped the Greeks express the complex and multifaceted nature of human love. They understood that love can take many forms, each with its own value and place in a well-rounded life. A harmonious blend of all seven forms of love is achievable in marital love throughout their journey together. As they age, erotic love may lessen, and in later years, love may become more about care and support, similar to early childhood. Together, these seven forms represent all types of love.

Distinction between Loving and Liking

Liking is frequently confused with loving, leading to the perception that being liked equates to being loved, or at the very least, receiving assurance of love. Elaine Hat Field and William Walster propose that liking and companionate love share significant similarities. "Liking is merely the fondness we have for casual acquaintances. Companionate love represents the affection we hold for those with whom our lives are profoundly connected." The primary distinction between liking and loving lies in the intensity of one's emotions and the extent of their engagement with the other individual.

- **Liking**

  Liking is a natural, emotional response, often beyond our control, like a reflex. People are usually drawn to others who are similar to them or complement them. Liking is influenced by the rewards someone provides—such as boosting self-esteem, sharing interests, or making one feel valued and understood.

  People tend to like others for specific qualities—physical, mental, social, or emotional—that they admire. This creates a sense of comfort and compatibility. However, liking is not as deep as love; losing someone you like may cause sadness, but it does not deeply disrupt your life, and there are no strong expectations from the person you like.

- **Loving**

  Loving is rooted in the will rather than in physical impulses. Liking is mutual, whereas love does not necessarily require reciprocity. Friends whom one claims to like may reciprocate those feelings, but a mother can love a rebellious son even if he does not reciprocate that love, as love transcends mere qualities. Loving is easy when affection is mutual; however, it becomes challenging when love is unreturned.

  Rubin (1973) characterized love as comprising three essential components.

  i. *Caring:* the feelings that another person's satisfactions are as important to one as his own.

  ii. *Attachment:* the yearning or desire to be in the presence of the other, to establish physical contact, and to receive approval and care.

  iii. *Intimacy:* the connection or bond shared between two individuals, which is demonstrated through close and confidential communication.

To illustrate the distinction between love and liking, Rubin administered his love and liking scales to 182 dating couples. Each participant completed the scales independently and confidentially alongside their partner. Subsequently, they were asked to fill out the scales a second time with a same-sex friend. The intriguing outcome of this research is as follows.

Initially, both friends and lovers were generally well-liked; however, friends did not achieve high scores on the love scale. Another unexpected finding is that, contrary to the common belief that women are more romantic than men, no significant differences were observed between males and females regarding the level of love expressed for their partners. Nevertheless, females demonstrated a greater expression of love towards their same-sex friends. This finding reinforces the notion that female same-sex friendships tend to be closer and more intimate than those among males. Usually, males express love feelings only in opposite sex relationships.

Individuals desire to be appreciated for their intrinsic qualities rather than solely for their ability to provide pleasure. However, emotions or feelings often fail to capture the profound essence of goodness that defines a person. Thus, it is love, rather than mere liking, that possesses the capacity to appreciate and accept the entirety of an individual. For one to truly feel loved, it is essential that someone genuinely likes them. Since liking is akin to love, it can be considered a close relative. Love necessitates commitment, which is distinct from liking. Commitment requires ongoing availability and loyalty within a relationship.

When an individual moves from merely liking someone to genuinely loving, that person becomes significant, and whose presence in one's life becomes immensely important. Due to the intimacy inherent in love, the absence of the beloved creates a deep void in one’s existence. The following lines by Smokey Robinson encapsulate this sentiment.

"I don't like you, but I love you; it seems that I'm always thinking of you.

Though you treat me badly, I love you madly.

You really got a hold on me."

To love deeply and sincerely, to like and care for another over an extended period, is a remarkable gift that humans can offer each other.

3

Love in Emotional Maturation

The term emotion is derived from the Latin verb "*motere,*" which means "to move," with the prefix "e-" indicating "move away." Every emotion tends to provoke a response. An emotion can be described as a patterned bodily reaction involving production, destruction, reproduction, deprivation, incorporation, rejection, exploration, or orientation, or a combination of these, triggered by a stimulus.

Danish physiologist Carl G. Lange stated, "An emotion is the way the body feels when there is a disturbed internal state, accompanied by various overt expressive movements." An emotional state can be defined as a reaction to external or internal stimuli that involves extensive bodily changes, the sensations of which create a backdrop against which the object or mental process that elicits the emotional state is perceived.

The emotion of love undergoes several phases before reaching adolescence. In the first three years, a child exhibits little or no sexual interest. It is a neutral period. Between the ages of 3 and 5, the child begins to show an increasing interest in sex, although sex and love operate independently during this time. At adolescence, the sexual instinct and the emotion of love become intertwined, leading the individual to "fall in love." This development occurs as the sexual organs and secondary sexual characteristics approach maturity.

The Phases of Maturing in Love

From birth until the sixth month, the child perceives itself as the primary love object. This phase is called as the auto-erotic period, during which the child is focused on bodily sensations such as stroking, petting, and holding. Excessive or insufficient petting may result in a persistent fixation of the child's affection on itself, leading to *narcissistic love.* Narcissistic love refers to a form of love that is self-centred and primarily focused on the individual's own needs, desires, and self-image rather than genuine care or empathy for the other person. It is fundamentally different from healthy, reciprocal love. Narcissists may express affection or say "I love you," but their feelings are often conditional, self-serving, and fleeting.

From approximately the sixth month to the end of the first year, the child's love shifts to the mother, who provides these sensations. This attachment continues until the age of eight in boys. Concurrently, around the age of four, there is an expansion of affection, where the boy begins to associate a teacher (or another figure) with the mother. This expansion of affection is crucial for the healthy development of the child's love life.

As the child approaches five years of age, the father emerges as the primary love object. By the age of ten, the boy's interest begins to shift towards peers of the same age and gender (friendship). Between the ages of 12 and 15, the gang age emerges. Around fifteen, there is a gradual transition towards individuals of the opposite sex who are of a similar age. Additionally, the boy may develop affection for an older individual. To ensure the normal progression of his love life, the boy must navigate through all these stages.

Emotional Development in Boys

As the boy child enters a phase of psychosexual development, he forms a particularly strong attachment to his mother, which is of an erotic nature. His desire to possess her leads to his father becoming a significant obstacle. Despite his deep affection for his father, he wishes for his father's removal, even to the extent of wishing for his death. This phenomenon is widely recognized as the ***Oedipus complex***, named after Oedipus, the king of Thebes, who unknowingly killed his father and married his mother. This concept was introduced by Sigmund Freud. It refers to a child's unconscious desire for the opposite - sex parent, typically occurring during the phallic stage (around 3-6 years old). For the boys this means: The desire for their mother, feelings of rivalry with their father. Sigmund Freud believed that resolving the Oedipus complex is crucial for healthy psychological development.

The initial hostility that the boy experiences towards his father is typically outgrown as he begins to emulate him. This occurs due to the boy's identification with his father. He may even seek a partner resembling the type of woman his father chose. Undoubtedly, a father plays a crucial role in shaping one's romantic life.

Emotional Development in Girls

Emotional maturation follows a similar path for girls as it does for boys. It is also important to note that the overall acceleration of development in girls begins even before birth. On average, girls exhibit greater maturity than boys at birth, and there is some evidence suggesting that they are often born after a shorter gestation period compared to boys.

During infancy, it is crucial to avoid excessive pampering or handling, which includes unnecessary carrying of the baby. There should be no undue emphasis on the child's physical appearance or the type of clothing they wear. If this is not adhered to, during adolescence, the girl may become solely focused on herself. She often spends hours in front of the mirror, feeling more wonderful than anyone else. This behaviour is referred to as a *narcissistic* attitude, characterized by an abnormal and excessive love or admiration for oneself.

A female child's bond with her father is understood through the lens of the ***Electra complex***. The Electro Complex is a psychological concept introduced by Carl Jung, inspired by the ancient Greek myth of Electra. It refers to a young girl's unconscious desire for her father and feelings of rivalry with her mother. The Electro complex is thought to occur during the phallic stage of development (around three to six years old), where a girl may experience attachment to her father, jealousy towards her mother and desire for her father's attention and affection.

The father's refusal to accept the transfer of affection around the age of six can lead to a fixation on the mother. Consequently, during adolescence, the girl may either completely submit to her mother's authority or rebel against it with such intensity that she seeks affection in the opposite direction. By the age of fifteen, a girl's interest in boys should have emerged; if not, it may indicate that her development is not progressing at a normal rate.

Typically, a girl will direct her first affections towards a prominent figure in her community or nation, with film stars often serving as common inspirations for developing emotions. Between the ages of fifteen and eighteen, the father becomes the primary object of affection for girls. The extension of affection towards older men outside the home may reflect a sense of identification with the father figure. As these young girls mature, they may find themselves falling in love with individuals who closely resemble their fathers.

Emotional Deprivation

The phrase 'emotional deprivation' denotes a deficiency, in a child's experience, of a positive reciprocal relationship with another individual. This emotional deprivation can significantly impact the development of the ability to engage in reciprocal love relationships. This emotional deprivation arises not only from a lack of nurturing care from the mother/father but also from insufficient environmental and social stimulation.

The type of stimulation that an infant typically and naturally receives from the continuous care and interaction with its mother is arguably the most suitable and effective stimulation for healthy emotional development. The research conducted by Harlow (1966), Marquis (1941), and Rhein Gold (1956) suggests that adequately addressing the infant's need for suitable stimulation and maternal care is fundamental for the development of emotional capacity. The ability to connect with others consistently in a mutually satisfying and supportive manner, as well as the capacity to love, are indicators of emotional maturity.

Love in the Freudian Stages of Psycho-Sexual Development

Stage	Type of Love	Primary Focus
Oral	Dependency, Trust, Need-based Love	Mother/caregiver as first love object
Anal	Control, Approval-Seeking	Boundaries and autonomy
Phallic	Sexualized Love (Oedipal/Electra)	Parent-focused desire and rivalry
Latency	Platonic Love, Friendship	Peer bonding and sublimation
Genital	Mature Romantic Love	Intimacy, sexuality, and partnership

1. Oral Stage (Birth – 1 year)

In the oral stage, an infant's pleasure centres around the mouth—through sucking, feeding, and exploring the world orally. Love during this stage is experienced primarily through the bond with the mother or primary caregiver. This is the first relationship a child forms, where trust, comfort, and dependency are key components. If the child receives consistent, nurturing care, they develop a basic sense of trust and emotional security—foundations for future loving relationships. However, fixation at this stage may result in an excessive need for oral stimulation (e.g., smoking, overeating) or an overdependence on others for emotional satisfaction in adult relationships.

2. Anal Stage (1 - 3 years)

The anal stage centres on the control of bodily functions, especially during toilet training. Love here is connected to the developing tension between autonomy and parental approval. The way a child navigates demands for control and cleanliness shapes their attitude toward authority, responsibility, and interpersonal dynamics. If this stage is resolved positively, the child learns to balance giving and withholding—an important skill in loving relationships. However, fixation can lead to either excessive control (anal-retentive) or chaotic behaviour (anal-expulsive) in relationships. Love may become conditional or tied to control, potentially causing power struggles in adult intimacy.

3. Phallic Stage (3 - 6 years)

During the phallic stage, the child becomes aware of their own genitals and begins to develop unconscious desires toward the opposite-sex parent—what Freud termed the *Oedipus complex* for boys and the *Electra complex* (a later adaptation by Jung) for girls. Love here is intertwined with early sexual feelings, competition, and gender identity. Successful resolution involves identifying with the same-sex parent, helping the child internalize adult gender roles and moral values. If fixation occurs—due to either overindulgence or harsh rejection—adult relationships may be marked by confusion around sexual identity, intimacy issues, or difficulty forming mature, reciprocal romantic attachments.

4. Latency Stage (6 – 12 years)

In the latency stage, sexual impulses are repressed, and energy is redirected toward socialization, learning, and building friendships. Love during this period is not romantic or sexual but instead expressed through affection, loyalty, and platonic bonding with peers, teachers, and same-sex role models. This stage is essential for developing emotional intelligence, empathy, and cooperative behaviours. These social skills lay the groundwork for future romantic love by fostering the ability to connect with others, communicate feelings, and build trust outside the family unit.

5. Genital Stage (12 years and onward)

The genital stage marks the return of the libido with a focus on mature, adult sexuality and love. Unlike the self-centred sexual curiosity of the earlier phallic stage, love here becomes other-oriented, involving emotional intimacy, empathy, and mutual satisfaction. If all previous stages have been successfully navigated, the individual can now form healthy, balanced romantic and sexual relationships. Love in the genital stage reflects psychological maturity, where one can give and receive love in a stable, committed, and emotionally fulfilling way.

Two Major Divisions of Love

However, not all forms of love are identical. One does not love his mother in the same manner as he loves girlfriends or boyfriends, or siblings. Researchers have proposed that there are indeed various types of love, categorized into two primary kinds. The first is companionate love, which encompasses love for parents, family members, and friends. The second is passionate love, which pertains to romantic love.

Companionate Love

Companionate love refers to the profound affection and bond that an individual feels for those who are significantly integrated into their life. This form of love encompasses intimacy and respect. It is founded on friendship, mutual attraction, shared interests, mutual respect, and a genuine concern for each other's happiness and well-being.

Passionate Love

Passionate love represents a powerful emotional experience that one perceives within their body. It is marked by a blend of emotions: tenderness and sexuality, joy and suffering, anxiety and relief, altruism and jealousy. Passionate love is frequently an unrealistic emotional reaction to another individual; those involved often perceive their feelings as "true love," while outside observers may categorize their response as "infatuation."

Part Three
Companionate Love

Companionate love emerges in relationships with those to whom one is closely connected. Parental love, affection for siblings, and the love found in friendships all fall under this category. This third part illustrates the significance of parental love in an individual's life, the lasting effects it has, and its role in shaping self-love and self-esteem. Additionally, the nature of friendship love is also addressed here. Both parental love and friendship love play distinct roles in adolescent romantic relationships. Therefore, comprehending these two forms of love is crucial prior to engaging in romantic love.

1
Parental Love

Parental love is fundamental and serves as the foundation for all other relationships. A lack of parental love can lead to challenges in future romantic relationships. Just as one cannot appreciate music without first being acquainted with it, the deeper one's love for it, the greater the understanding. Where does the love of virtue originate in a child's heart if it is not already instilled by the parent? Holman states, "The most potent influence in child culture is imitation." A child embodies the subtle impressions of their home environment. If that environment is filled with love, the child will absorb it.

The Significant Role of Parental Love

Parental love plays a crucial role in the development of an individual's personality. Karen Horney (Psychologist, 1937) proposed that personality evolves through social interactions, particularly emphasizing the bond between parents and their children and the extent to which the child's needs are fulfilled. Some children may receive substantial gifts (such as cakes, clothing, toys, money, etc.) yet still feel unloved. This feeling arises from a lack of genuine belonging. They may intuitively sense that their parents are withholding their true selves while providing material items.

Children do not require possessions; rather, they need the love of their parents. A child devoid of material wealth but surrounded by the warmth of parental affection is significantly happier than a materially rich child who possesses everything. While money can procure items, it cannot provide the essential security that comes from being genuinely loved.

Rollo May asserts that individuals who lack love and trust during infancy may develop a schizoid personality, characterized by emotional detachment and an aversion to close relationships, leading to an inability to experience feelings. Antony Storr notes that those with a schizoid personality often believe they are unlovable and feel attacked and humiliated by criticism. When something is deemed valuable, it is cherished, nurtured, and cared for. Similarly, the belief in one's own value (I am a valuable person) is vital for mental well-being and serves as a foundation for self-esteem. This belief must be instilled during childhood, as it is exceedingly challenging to cultivate in adulthood.

Adolescents across various families have expressed, in various ways, the significance of their parents' love. Some articulated this sentiment directly, while others exhibited resentment and misbehaviour when they perceived their parents as having failed or abandoned them. Parents often view their children as extensions of themselves, akin to possessions (such as cars, televisions, houses, etc.), neglecting to recognize the unique individuality of their children. Khalil Gibran articulates some of the most profound words ever penned regarding the upbringing of children.

"*Your children are not your children.*
They are the sons and daughters of life's longing for itself..."

It is indeed the case that when discipline is excessively harsh, the negative emotions of shame, fear, inferiority, and guilt may become prevalent, potentially leading to a tendency to withdraw in interpersonal relationships.

The Importance of Loving One's Parents

An adolescent who appreciates their parents and embodies good character feels reciprocated love, experiences happiness and satisfaction within the relationship, possesses high self-esteem, trusts others, and demonstrates prosocial behaviour. Jeffries (1993) posits that the love for one's parents is founded on both *attraction* and *virtue*. Here, virtue is defined as a person's goodness, characterized by moral and ethical behaviour.

Attraction towards parents involves feelings of respect and admiration, enjoyment of shared time, reliance on their honesty and integrity, willingness to self-disclose, and sharing of personal concerns, as well as empathy for their joys and sorrows. Virtue in children includes assisting, forgiving, and tolerating their parents, advocating for their benefit, fulfilling obligations, respecting their rights, enduring hardships for their sake, managing disruptive emotions, and practicing self-discipline. To cultivate and sustain a loving relationship with parents, one must accept them as they are. A crucial aspect of any parent-child relationship is the maintenance of open communication. Achieving this foster mutual understanding, respect, empathy, and honesty.

Attachment In Infancy - Adult Loving Style

Psychologist Phillip Shaver and his colleagues have noted that the attachment styles formed during infancy persist into adulthood, influencing romantic relationships. Infants are typically categorized into three attachment styles: Securely attached (children who enjoy a healthy, positive, and trusting relationship); Avoidant (infants who show indifference towards caregivers and tend to avoid interactions with them); and anxious-ambivalent (infants who experience significant distress when separated from a caregiver but exhibit anger upon the caregiver's return).

Adults with a *secure attachment style* generally find it easier to enter into relationships and feel optimistic and confident about the future of these relationships. They rarely worry about abandonment or about someone becoming too close to them. The majority of young adults—slightly over half—exhibit a secure attachment style (Hazan & Shaver, 1987).

Adults with an *avoidant attachment style* often feel uncomfortable with intimacy; they struggle to trust and rely on others. They tend to feel anxious when someone gets too close, experience higher rates of break-ups, and frequently feel lonely.

Adults with an *anxious-ambivalent attachment style* are somewhat uncomfortable in being close to others and find it difficult to trust and depend on them. They are nervous when anyone gets too close and have higher breakup rates and often feel lonely. They frequently worry that their partner does not genuinely love them or wish to remain with them. They have a strong desire to fully merge with others, which can sometimes intimidate people (Shaver, Hazan & Bradshaw, 1988). This group tends to become excessively invested in relationships, experiences repeated break-ups with the same partner, and often has relatively low self-esteem. Approximately 20 percent of adults fall into this category (Simpson, 1990).

It is evident that there are continuities between the attachment styles formed in infancy and adult behaviour. Individuals facing challenges in their relationships may benefit from reflecting on their early attachment experiences to uncover the underlying causes of their difficulties (Brennan & Shaver, 1995).

Mother's Love

The mother is typically one of the first individuals with whom an infant establishes a relationship. The infant plays a crucial role in the process of developing this relationship. The manner in which a mother and infant cultivate their bond is dynamic, reciprocal, and vital for the child's future. The positive emotional connection that forms between a child and a specific individual represents the most significant form of social development that takes place during infancy (Greeberg, Ciccnetti & Cummings, 1990).

The Mother Complex

The nature of the early relationship with the mother significantly influences the type of mother complex that a boy will carry into adulthood. If this relationship is warm and nurturing, the boy feels loved and accepted, leading to the development of a *positive mother complex*. His conscious belief becomes, "My mother loved me; if others do not, there must be something wrong with them." Consequently, such a boy is likely to feel a strong connection to and appreciation for women and femininity. Conversely, if the relationship is negative and rejecting, the boy may feel unwanted and unloved, resulting in a *negative mother complex*. He may reach maturity with a lack of self-confidence, embodying the role of an "injured child." As an adult, he may develop distrust towards women and struggle to form healthy relationships. To avoid further emotional pain, he is likely to build unconscious emotional barriers between himself and his partner or spouse. Additionally, the negative mother complex may instil the feelings of guilt and self-rejection within him.

It is indeed tragic for a child to be born without the care of two parents who can provide security in a nurturing home. Regardless of how much a mother may love her child and desire to care for it, she cannot fulfil the role of both father and mother. Maternal deprivation can lead to emotional damage during infancy, prompting the child to seek out someone else who can provide the loving care he missed, which may result in romantic relationships with women in adulthood.

Feelings of Unwantedness

One hypothesis is that the foetus's autonomic nervous system becomes particularly sensitive due to the chemical alterations stemming from the mother's emotional state. Therefore, it is essential for pregnant women to embrace and love their foetus. If a mother perceives her foetus as unwanted, this perception can instil feelings of unwantedness within the foetus, leading to challenges in future relationships, particularly in romantic contexts.

The mother's sentiments regarding an unwanted pregnancy may be internalized by the developing baby, resulting in the child experiencing a sense of worthlessness, especially during early adolescence. As an adult, this individual may grapple with the 'unwanted' message from their mother, potentially leading to suicidal ideation characterized by thoughts such as 'I want to die' or 'Why should I live?' Furthermore, it is noted that 'psychopaths who lack an understanding of affection often come from backgrounds with minimal maternal love.' Erickson (1968) indicates that early parent-child interactions that either foster or hinder a sense of trust in one's environment, such as the care provided by a nurturing figure during infancy who is 'warmly dependable,' may contribute to the emergence of a challenging identity crisis.

Physical Contact and Emotional Development

For an extended period, it was thought that the affection and dependence exhibited by infants stemmed from the connection between the mother and the fulfilment of physical needs, particularly in relation to feeding. Psychologists, sociologists, and anthropologists generally agree that an infant's love is cultivated through the association of the mother's facial features, body, and other physical traits with the relief of internal biological pressures, especially hunger and thirst. Psychologists have posited that the act of nursing and suckling at the breast serves as the foundation for emotional development.

Harry Harlow (1950) conducted research on Rhesus infant monkeys at the private Laboratory of the University of Wisconsin. The findings underscore the significance of physical contact and the immediate comfort it provides in establishing the infant's attachment to its mother. This does not imply that nursing lacks psychological significance. However, Harlow (1962) discovered that monkeys raised without maternal contact later exhibited minimal interest in the opposite sex. Consequently, he proposed that the instinctual need for physical contact outweighs the importance of food rewards (this is also applicable to human infants).

In terms of emotional needs, the baby is born and relies completely on its mother for survival. To ensure this, it develops an emotional bond with her, referred to as emotional attachment. The mother cradles the baby, and touch becomes a potent means of fostering intimacy. This capacity to form attachments is fundamental to all human relationships.

Overprotected - Childhood

Individuals who experienced excessive protection during their formative years often learned that appearing to be ill was an effective way to secure love and attention from others; consequently, they may develop psychosomatic disorders in response to stress. (A psychosomatic disorder is a condition where psychological factors like stress, anxiety, or depression can cause or worsen physical symptoms).

The American behaviourist psychologist J.B. Watson concurs with Freud's assertion that excessive "parental tenderness spoils the child," leading to challenges later in life when the individual must cope with diminished affection. When a mother keeps her son within a sphere where she is the focal point, it results in an infantile fixation that hinders the boy's ability to engage in normal romantic relationships.

According to Symonds (1939), an overabundance of maternal acceptance, characterized by exaggerated displays of love and concern, may serve as an unconscious compensation for or a shield against her fundamental rejection and lack of authentic affection for him. This superficial acceptance of a child reflects the emotional immaturity of the parent. I.D. Harris (1959) posits that the overt 'love' expressed is not true love for the child, but rather an exploitation of the child as part of the parents' unconscious self-serving attempts to fulfil their own unmet emotional needs. These dynamics stem from the parents' own childhood experiences within their families.

Possessive Mother

All mothers who exhibit excessive possessiveness and struggle to let go of a loved one must recognize that such love can become a burden when it is not reciprocated. The mother desires to make sacrifices for those she cherishes, yet she may fall into self-deception if her love is rejected. Some adults feel hindered in their emotional development as long as their mother's overwhelming, protective love envelops them. While love fosters connection, possessiveness can lead to destruction.

The possessive mother does not truly love her child; rather, she suppresses her child by undermining his ability to develop into an independent individual and lead his own life. He may also unconsciously compete for the father's affection, especially if the love dynamic between the parents is unstable. The mother's Eros may overly bind the son to her, potentially resulting in sexual difficulties later in life, and in extreme cases, contributing to homosexuality. Consequently, he may struggle to form a lasting relationship with another woman.

Father's Love

Robert Bly asserts that boys experience a "body-longing" for their fathers. If this need remains unmet during adulthood, the individual may yearn for masculine affection, which can sometimes lead to homosexuality. When two mature men embrace and cuddle as a small boy would with his father, it is labelled as homosexuality. A father who holds negative views towards feminine qualities may undermine his daughter's creative spirit as it begins to emerge. This can lead her to feel unlovable to men. In one instance, a woman whose father neglected her developed intense erotic fantasies of being wholly loved by a man; however, her initial experiences with men were starkly opposite, involving encounters with those who devalued her and left her feeling more wounded than before. While she yearned for a man's affection, she found herself increasingly resentful towards men, drawn to replicate the same rejection she faced in her childhood relationships.

Symptoms of Loss of Parental Affection

The individual who does not receive adequate love from their parent may exhibit the following symptoms: a naturally quick temper, aggressive emotional expressions, a tendency to be hypercritical of authority, diminished concern for others, an inability to express affection, inadequacy in intimate relationships, a mechanical approach to sexuality, poor interpersonal relationships, and calculated retaliation against those who offend them.

Relationships Between and Among Siblings

For approximately 80 percent of children grow up with at least one sibling. The interactions with the siblings facilitate the practice of interpersonal skills. Brothers and sisters frequently experience a blend of emotions - including affection, rivalry, and hostility. Siblings can be both a source of annoyance to one another and fierce competitors. They compete for the attention and affection of their parents. Sibling rivalry is so prevalent that it is regarded as a normal aspect of growing up. The emotions triggered by sibling interactions persist throughout one's life in other relationships, as friendships, romantic relationships, and marriages often elicit reactions that were originally associated with siblings (Klagsbrum, 1992).

2
Self-Love

The first entity that a child love is itself. Infants are initially incapable of loving anyone else. They are unaware that there are other individuals to love. At first, the child loves itself in a very basic manner, such as enjoying its fingers and sucking on them with delight. As the child becomes aware of itself as a distinct individual, some degree of self-love is natural. Furthermore, during adolescence, a certain level of self-preoccupation is typical. However, loving oneself does not mean placing oneself above others, boasting, or being egotistical. Rather, it involves seeking and nurturing the positive aspects within oneself.

While the love shared between two different individuals is comprehensible, the most challenging form of love to grasp is self-love. The phrase "know yourself" has been a fundamental goal of human understanding since ancient times. Bertrand Russell once stated, "A man cannot possibly be at peace with others until he has learned to be at peace with himself." Rabbi Joshua Liebman has suggested a reinterpretation of the biblical commandment of love, proposing that it should read: "Love and believe in yourself properly, and you will love and believe in your neighbour." Erich Fromm (1956) remarked, "Love, in principle, is indivisible concerning the connection between 'objects' and one's own self."

Love Yourself

Essentially, to love oneself entails being in harmony with and within oneself. This requires that one's authentic "self" governs their entire existence. A person's life is considered to be in order when they do not permit their desires and emotions to overpower them. If the 'I' manages the controllable aspects of one's being, then true self-love is present. Conversely, if the 'I' is not in command, but rather a specific part is, then true self-love has not yet been achieved. In such circumstances, one cannot fully surrender their entire self to another.

Love does not pursue its own interests. Given this reality, love seems to counteract one of the most profound instincts within any healthy individual—the instinct to seek out and become one's ideal self. Thus, self-seeking is essential. However, in the book 'The Miracle of Mind Power,' Dan Custer asserts that it is both normal and appropriate for an individual to first love themselves, and subsequently extend that love to their neighbour, as no one can reconcile with life unless they first reconcile with themselves. An individual will find it impossible to love others until they have first loved themselves. Therefore, self-seeking is indeed necessary.

Distinction Between Selfishness and Self-Love

Love represents an expansion, a reaching out beyond oneself. Selfishness, on the other hand, is the affection for a misguided self; specifically, the self that diverges from the feelings, interests, and safety of others. Erich Fromm, in his work 'Escape from Freedom,' states, "Selfishness is not synonymous with self-love, but rather its complete antithesis. Selfishness is a form of greed. Like all forms of greed, it embodies an insatiable nature, resulting in a perpetual state of dissatisfaction… selfishness is rooted in a fundamental lack of affection for oneself."

Narcissism, akin to selfishness, serves as an excessive response to the fundamental absence of self-love. The term originates from the ancient Greek tale of Narcissus, who fell in love with his own reflection in a tranquil pool of water. He cherished his image to such an extent that he withered away and perished, leading to the emergence of the flower that bears his name, which marks his burial site. Today, when an individual loves and admires himself, he is often labelled as narcissistic; however, such a person truly loves neither others nor himself.

Loving Oneself While Loving Others

According to Aristotle, "Men must by their very nature love themselves even when loving others." Aristotle referred to this as self-realization, asserting that individuals are at their most moral when they strive to realize their true selves. Erich Fromm stated that one's highest calling is to "take loving care of himself." Self-love transcends merely enjoying the thrill of being a remarkable person, as love elevates one's aspirations beyond the ideal self that one is pursuing.

Mature Self-Love

Mature self-love does not involve merely praising oneself or declaring oneself a wonderful person. It is not simply about prioritizing one's own needs over those of others. Instead, mature self-love encompasses a spirit that is interwoven throughout and governs one's entire being. This should represent the natural progression of personality development. Dr. Robert H. Felix, the former director of the National Institute for Mental Health, characterizes this healthy love and acceptance of oneself as a "feeling of dignity, belonging, worthwhileness, and adequacy." Thus, self-love fundamentally equates to self-respect and self-trust. An individual possessing these qualities is prepared to both give and receive love that is centred on others.

The most selfless love anticipates and hopes for a reciprocation of love, as other-centred love is inherently reciprocal, and the lover appreciates the warm generosity of the beloved. Conversely, if the lover demands a response from the beloved in an imperious manner, it may restrict the beloved's freedom, leading to a situation where self-love becomes selfish and unhealthy, as the focus shifts from giving to receiving from the beloved.

Self-Love and Self Esteem

Self-esteem is essential for effective human communication. Dr. Huntley states, "Other individuals respond to you based on the verbal and non-verbal signals you convey about yourself." Self-esteem originates from self-love, which is a product of healthy parental affection. Children learn how to feel about themselves from how their parents treat them. If they aren't shown love, they may grow up with low self-esteem. If love is inconsistent, they may learn to show only the parts of themselves that get approval.

Thus, an individual who has genuinely experienced love from their parents and other significant figures in their life can develop a sense of self-love. If a person does not feel lovable, they cannot believe that anyone desires to know them, establish a relationship with them, or love them. Such individuals struggle to accept themselves and may feel worthless. These are the individuals in society who find it difficult to form meaningful relationships.

Self-love is crucial for allowing others to approach us and reflects one's capacity to embrace the positive feelings of others. It enables an individual to feel good about themselves, fostering trust in their ability to provide positive contributions to others. The experience of unconditional acceptance from one's parents serves as the foundation for self-love and self-esteem. Authentic self-esteem is grounded in a realistic evaluation of one's own abilities and intrinsic worth.

An Empty Person

The individual who has neither loved nor been loved is considered an empty person and, in this emptiness, lacks genuine love for himself. He experiences feelings of rejection, insecurity, fear, discouragement, self-deprecation, failure, envy, and jealousy. Furthermore, he struggles to accept authentic love from others. Thus, a person who does not love himself may cope with his situation by becoming a critic of others, constantly identifying and highlighting their flaws. Naturally, his criticisms are essentially self-accusations, although he remains unaware of this fact. His critical stance is rooted in a projection of his self-perception. Lacking a sense of personal worth, he bases his assumed value solely on his performance. Consequently, when something undesirable occurs, he is unwilling to acknowledge his mistakes. Admitting his faults and failures would entail too much emotional pain. Such an individual is a perfectionist, believing that performance is a prerequisite for recognition and love.

He fears criticism from others, their evaluations of him, and ultimately their rejection. One method of coping with this painful state of emptiness is to portray oneself in such a negative light that others will have low expectations and may even offer sympathy. He strives to be a pleasant person at all times, ensuring absolute agreeability. Additionally, traits such as anger, an overachieving tendency, introjections, cynicism, suspicion, and timidity characterize an empty person.

One can only know oneself through the reflections seen in the eyes of others. Therefore, one's fundamental sense of self-appreciation is largely a gift from his parents. The essential human need is to possess a true and profound love for oneself, leading to genuine and joyful self-acceptance and authentic self-esteem, which culminates in an internal sense of celebration: "It's good to be me... I am very happy to be me!"

When the worthiness of love becomes contingent upon passing tests and meeting conditions, one begins to encounter repeated failures, resulting in conflict, fear, frustration, pain, and ultimately some form of self-hatred. Thus, he dedicates the remainder of his life to evading this anguish through the means previously described. In doing so, he relinquishes his true self in favour of becoming someone else, someone deemed deserving of acknowledgment and affection.

3
The Love of Friendship

Human beings are inherently social creatures. They seek the presence of others. They desire to love someone and to be loved in return. Life resembles a roller-coaster journey in the dark, filled with numerous highs and lows, leaving one uncertain of what lies ahead. Therefore, it is essential to ensure that one is accompanied by someone they appreciate and trust.

Paul Tournier once remarked, "No one can develop freely in this world and find a full life without feeling understood by at least one person." Consequently, genuine friendship holds significant value for all individuals. Friends have the ability to enhance difficult moments and elevate joyful occasions. The friendships cultivated throughout one's life represent some of the most crucial relationships they will ever encounter, and it is vital for their happiness and well-being to nurture these connections.

Establishing a bond requires time, from the initial meeting to the moment one realizes they have discovered someone they can trust and who reciprocates that trust. Friendship is an intensely personal experience, and only the individual who claims another adult as a friend can truly define it. Therefore, the subsequent definitions may provide insight into the essence of friendship.

Friendly Relationship

A friend is described as "one loving or attached to another". Furthermore, it is said, "Friendship is a powerful tie of a deeper and more lasting kind—an intimate union of two persons by the bond of love". In its noun form, a friend can also be described as an intimate, confidant, supporter, sympathizer, backer, comrade, companion, partner, chum, or buddy, and can be distinguished by gender as a girlfriend or boyfriend. A friendly relationship typically suggests that a friend is kind, sympathetic, responsive, affectionate, cordial, understanding, sociable, agreeable, and intimate.

Friendship represents a type of relationship between individuals, whether they are of the same or opposite sex. It is characterized by mutual understanding and acceptance, along with a strong sense of encouragement. In this bond, individuals are willing to share each other's burdens and are prepared to make significant sacrifices, even to the extent of risking their own lives. There are no barriers of age, talent, gender, size, beauty, or wealth. In essence, "there will be two bodies but only one soul".

Friendship embodies an act of love where there is a free and mutual exchange of the gift of self between two or more individuals. To cultivate a love known as friendship, both parties must possess a sufficient understanding of their inner selves to altruistically reach out to one another. The concept of friendship is subjective, varying according to individual perception. The notion that like attracts like holds true in friendship. The essence of friendship lies in the special bond that two (or more) individuals share, where they genuinely enjoy each other's company and feel more comfortable with one another than with anyone else.

The Importance of Friendship

People with friends are generally healthier and happier, have less depression and anxiety, get sick less often, and tend to live longer, according to psychotherapist Lillian Rubin. "A friend sets aside his own plans when someone is in distress, celebrates one's achievements, and feels sorrow when one is suffering," states psychotherapist Doris Wild Helmering. A friend supports one's aspirations and provides guidance—but even if one chooses not to heed it, he continues to respect and love him.

Helen Keller remarked, "If one has friends, he can withstand anything." The German poet Goethe emphasizes the significance of friendship in the following verse: "The world is so barren if one only considers mountains, rivers, and cities, but to know someone who thinks and feels alongside me, and who, despite the distance, is close to me in spirit, transforms the earth into an inhabited garden for me."

Aristotle's Perspective on Friendship

Aristotle proposed a foundational hypothesis on friendship, asserting that individuals who share similar values and perspectives are more likely to form friendships, whereas those with fundamentally opposing views tend not to do so. This alignment of desires and judgments, according to Aristotle, forms the psychological basis of enduring interpersonal bonds. A similar idea was later articulated by Sallust in the Latin phrase *"Idem velle atque idem nolle, ea demum firma amicitia est,"* meaning, "To desire the same things and to reject the same things—this is true friendship."

Modern social psychology has provided empirical support for Aristotle's hypothesis, with numerous studies demonstrating that similarity in attitudes, beliefs, and values strongly predicts the formation and stability of friendships. Aristotle further maintained that the highest form of friendship is not merely based on shared opinions but on a shared commitment to living well. He famously asserted that living a good life for the sake of one's friends constitutes the essence of true friendship, emphasizing its moral and relational depth.

Building on this ethical framework, Aristotle classified friendship into three distinct types. **Friendship of utility** is formed for practical advantage, in which individuals associate with others to accomplish tasks or fulfill needs. **Friendship of pleasure** is based on enjoyment and emotional gratification derived from the other person. Both forms are inherently unstable, as they persist only as long as the utility or pleasure remains, and may therefore carry a degree of instrumental or manipulative motivation. In contrast, **friendship of virtue** is grounded in mutual respect, moral excellence, and a genuine concern for the other's well-being. This form of friendship is authentic, enduring, and central to human flourishing. It is worth recalling the words of Socrates, who once urged his followers to choose their friendships carefully, but once established, to remain steadfast and loyal.

Two Causes for The Emergence of Friendship

The initial cause involves recognizing a certain deficiency or lack within oneself, or a specific void that requires fulfilment. Upon encountering an object that appears to address this deficiency and fill the void, a desire to possess that object as a complement to one's life arises.

The second cause happens when a person, even without a strong initial desire, encounters an object that seems to present a new avenue for self-development; consequently, there is a desire to possess that object as it contributes to a new perfection of one's being. When people have different traits, their friendship is often based on meeting each other's needs, as each person complements the other. When people are similar, the friendship is more likely based on helping each other grow and develop further.

Childhood Friendship

Childhood friendships are formed when two children discover mutual enjoyment in engaging in similar activities. Even toddlers as young as one or two years can forge enduring relationships. During childhood, children cultivate both casual friendships and close bonds with a singular individual. By approximately the age of three, children begin to form genuine friendships. The essence of this friendship lies in the enjoyment of shared activities, collaborative endeavours, and joint play. However, a close friendship is esteemed for qualities such as generosity, sensitivity, and honesty (Urbanski, 1992).

Close friendship is characterized as "A relationship in which friends spend a significant amount of time together, interact in various situations, exclude others from the relationship, and provide emotional support to one another." The dynamics of interpersonal relationships and the child's attachment style with their mother significantly influence how they interact, thereby impacting childhood friendships.

Friendship Among Adolescents and Adults

The friendships that adults form may fulfil various purposes, including intimacy, admiration, ego enhancement, identification, dependency needs, decision-making, encouragement, providing solace during times of sorrow, providing feedback, and alleviating loneliness, even if one does not have a strong fondness for the friend. This type of friendship is characterized by greater intimacy compared to childhood friendships, with women reporting a higher number of close friends than men (Fredrickson, 1995).

An "intimate relationship" is defined as one in which both individuals feel at ease engaging in self-disclosure, expressing emotions, offering and receiving support, experiencing trust, engaging in physical contact, and generally feeling relaxed in each other's company. Friendly relationships with neighbours, as well as the criteria that define friendships, appear to stem from a man's relationship with himself.

A person with a positive self-image tends to feel comfortable in close relationships, whereas an individual with a negative self-image may fear rejection from others and experience feelings of anxiety, unworthiness, and dependency. This individual may be motivated to avoid close relationships due to the expectation that others will be unavailable and unsupportive. Consequently, a person lacking close relationships experiences loneliness, which is the emotional state resulting from the desire for close interpersonal connections that remain unattainable.

Friendship with the Opposite Sex

The essence of friendship, in its purest form, is typically found between individuals of the same gender. However, this does not imply that genuine friendships cannot develop between individuals of different genders; indeed, it is recognized that "Platonic love (a profound and intimate bond devoid of sexual elements) can exist between a man and a woman without any sexual components." This does not suggest that sexual love, which may lead to marriage, is incompatible with friendship; rather, marital love should encompass all aspects of friendship. It is through friendship that spouses can truly comprehend one another. If physical attraction initially draws a man and a woman together, it is only through friendship that they can truly understand each other as they are. Psychologically, this form of love is distinct from sexual love. The love of friendship is a spiritual connection, primarily emotional, while the sexual component (which may accompany friendship) is driven by instinct and is inherently passionate.

Friendship is rooted in the spiritual realm and is thus influenced by intellectual motives. However, when sexual elements are introduced, all rational considerations seem to dissipate. The intensity of passionate attachment can consume one's entire being, instilling a profound desire to overcome any challenges for the sake of the other. Instinct alone can account for this phenomenon. Therefore, friendship with the opposite sex can be beneficial and enriching until sexual elements complicate it.

Sensual Friendship or Particular Friendship

This type of friendship is characterized by a closeness akin to that of lovers. The individuals involved prefer not to engage with others. This can occur between two men, two women, or even between individuals of opposite sexes.

Indicators of Sensual Friendship

This type of friendship is characterized by exclusivity. This exclusivity is evident in the manner in which the two friends isolate themselves from others to enjoy each other's company, express annoyance when others intrude upon their time together, and exhibit jealousy to the extent of anger if one observes the other socializing with a third individual. Jealousy can manifest within a friendship; when a third party becomes a friend to one's friend but not to oneself, there arises a fear of losing a part of that friendship, leading to feelings of exclusion from shared experiences with the third party. This fear is what we term Jealousy. Christopher Bannister articulates, "Do not be envious of your friend's relationships with others; indeed, the more friends he possesses, the better friend he becomes to you."

Possessiveness can escalate to a level where one cannot bear the absence of the other, seeks to extend conversations and visits excessively, and tends to dominate the other individual. Sensual friendships can become obsessive, with friends constantly preoccupied with thoughts of one another, akin to young lovers. Consequently, they find it challenging to focus on anything else. There exists a strong desire to express affection. Given their close bond, there is a potential for the emergence of homosexual, lesbian, or illicit sexual relationships between them. To prevent such a friendship from developing, one must possess a firm belief in its detrimental nature and confidence in their ability to manage their emotions. Additionally, both physical and mental separations are essential.

Cultivating Friendship

Man is inherently a social creature who needs companionship and friendship throughout his life. Indeed, while the network of acquaintances may be extensive, the circle of true friends tends to be limited. Therefore, one must seek friendship in the unique qualities of individuals that elicit a special response from oneself. Developing friendships necessitates engaging with others and making a conscious effort to be social. A prominent psychiatrist states, "Integrating into a social group that mirrors our own identity is an essential aspect of personal growth. Isolation frequently leads to depression, which subsequently diminishes our inclination to socialize."

Many individuals form friendships, yet not all are successful in maintaining them. Often, people establish friendships and then anticipate that the relationship will naturally evolve. Contrary to popular belief, friendships do not simply occur by coincidence. One must actively nurture them. It requires initiative on one's part, as noted by Biju Punnathanam. Most importantly, Emerson asserts, "The only way to have a friend is to be one." Friendship represents the union of two distinct individuals, each with their own desires, talents, temperaments, experiences, and backgrounds. Thus, it demands sacrifice and understanding from both parties.

Determinations of Friendship

Much of the research conducted on friendship has employed a method known as 'sociometry'. The findings indicate that the more frequently individuals meet, the more they tend to like each other. The degree to which one person fulfils the needs of another influences their mutual affection. Consequently, Homans (1961) proposed that all social relationships resemble economic transactions or exchanges of gifts. Individuals with similar values and interests are likely to develop fondness for one another.

Another theory posits that opposites attract. Numerous studies suggest that dominant and submissive individuals may gravitate towards each other. People often select companions who can assist them in endeavours they struggle to manage independently. Within this interpersonal framework, interactions that foster liking may ultimately lead to genuine friendships.

Dale Carnegie states, "You make friends by becoming interested in other people rather than by attempting to interest others in yourself." Therefore, to cultivate authentic friendships, one must expand their social circle by engaging with new individuals from diverse backgrounds, accompanied by a genuine sense of enthusiasm and joy. It is essential to refrain from self-judgment and judgment of others, while providing constructive feedback in a way that encourages improvement.

Possessing a sense of humour, avoiding prejudices, being adaptable, attuning to the emotions of others and responding appropriately, fostering open communication, learning to listen, accepting a friend's individuality, maintaining contact, revisiting shared memories, allowing others the freedom to be themselves, respecting the feelings of others, and looking beyond conflicts will aid in the development of friendships. Friendship can be a source of ecstasy, yet it invariably carries the burden of profound suffering. Amidst the joy and pain, there exists an inexplicably beautiful and compelling aspect to it. It evokes a sense of the grandeur of an all-loving God.

True Friendship

Father Lacordaire (1802-61) once remarked that "true friendship is a divine gift, a clear indication of a noble spirit, and one of the most significant rewards of genuine virtue." Authentic friendship is characterized by understanding, forgiveness, generosity, sympathy, appreciation, and above all, love. True friendships are founded on mutual respect and sincere affection.

A true friend is loyal and genuinely concerned for his or her companion. True friendship represents a union of souls committed to doing good. It is devoid of duplicity or hypocrisy; it acknowledges the flaws present in friends, yet it allows them to love one another despite their imperfections and vulnerabilities. Its primary focus is not on one's own benefit, but rather on the welfare of the other.

Those who truly want what is best for their friends, for the friends' own sake, are the truest friends. However, some friends may be reluctant to correct their companions. The modern Western philosopher Francis Bacon stated, "Those friends are weak who do not exercise the privilege of friendship by admonishing their friends with freedom and confidence, regarding both their errors and their dangers."

According to St. Thomas Acquinas, friendship consists of three components: *Benevolence,* which is a profound desire for the good of the other, even at significant personal cost; *Mutual benevolence,* which implies that not only must the beloved exhibit benevolence, but the lover must also possess the humility to acknowledge his own incompleteness and need for love; and the *sharing* of a common life filled with vital activity, thought, desire, and creative purpose.

A person who is overly self-centred cannot show the kindness needed for deep friendship. Friendship is a bond between people at their best as individuals, and it separates them from the crowd, much like being alone—sometimes even more strongly, because it happens in small groups.

One must accept their friend as they are and refrain from criticizing them each time, they make mistakes. Interdependence promotes growth; however, the failure to recognize one's individuality apart from that of a friend can be detrimental. For a healthy friendship, it is crucial to regard the other as a distinct person rather than an extension of oneself. Characteristics of genuine friendship include commitment to one another, loyalty, mutual trust, selfless love, respect, forgiveness, confidentiality, sincere concern, and providing comfort in times of need.

Part Four
Passionate Love

It is inherently significant for a man to cultivate intimate relationships with individuals of both genders. Particularly, a bond with a woman serves as a crucible for a man, enhancing his self-awareness and revealing various facets of his personality. This is why Adolph Guggenbuhl remarked that "Marriage exists not for our well-being but for our salvation." When individuals express that they are in love, they typically refer to passionate love; however, love can manifest in several other forms. The following pages will elucidate the different theories associated with the experience of falling in love.

1
Love in the Teen Years

Psychologists Elaine Hatfield and Ellen Berscheid, elucidate in their Labelling theory of passionate love - why a person who continually faces rejection or emotional pain from another can still perceive themselves as "in love" with that individual? It is suggested that rejection induces physiological arousal, which is misinterpreted as "love," prompting individuals to conclude that they are even more in love than prior to experiencing such adverse emotions. This phenomenon likely occurs because the virtues of passion are celebrated in love songs, advertisements, television programs, and films.

A person experiencing passionate love is often consumed by the thoughts of their beloved, perceiving them as flawless or without imperfections. Even perceived faults in their partner are viewed as virtues. Passionate love appears to be a blend of sexual attraction, physiological arousal, a yearning for physical closeness, an intense desire to be loved in return, and a persistent anxiety regarding the potential end of the relationship. Consequently, the individual regards their partner as the ideal romantic companion and experiences profound despair at the thought of separation.

Love, especially in the teen years, is a powerful and transformative experience that shapes emotions, identity, and relationships in lasting ways. During adolescence, young people begin to explore deep feelings of attraction, attachment, and affection for the first time, often with an intensity that feels overwhelming yet meaningful. These early experiences of love are closely tied to personal growth, self-discovery, and emotional maturity. Though often misunderstood or dismissed as fleeting, teenage love plays a significant role in helping individuals understand trust, empathy, and the complexities of human connection.

Adolescent and Adulthood

Adolescence represents a transitional phase. During this time, an individual undergoes both physical and psychological changes, evolving from childhood into adulthood. The term "adolescence" is derived from the Latin words '*ad*' (to) and '*alescere*' (grow up), with the primary developmental objective of this stage being maturation. This period commences with the biological transformations associated with puberty. However, the duration of adolescence is influenced in part by cultural factors. Medically, it is recognized that adolescence initiates with the growth and hormonal shifts linked to sexual maturity and concludes when physical growth ceases. Psychologically, this phase is characterized by a transition during which cognitive, physical, personality, and social changes take place.

Boys aged 14 to 17 years and girls aged 13 to 17 years are classified as being in early adolescence or their teen years, commonly referred to as teenagers. The late adolescence phase typically spans ages 17 to 18, during which individuals are termed youths, followed by adulthood, which generally begins between the ages of 21 and 25 and extends to 40-60 years. Adulthood is further categorized into three stages: early, middle, and late adulthood. According to Erik H. Erikson, the psychological conflict during this period is *Intimacy vs Isolation*. A positive resolution leads to the formation of loving, sexual relationships and close friendships, while a negative outcome results in a fear of interpersonal relationships.

Adolescent and Sexual Drive

During the adolescent phase, boys experience a sex drive that is inherently erotic. As a result, they undergo significant sexual arousal and a heightened sense of tension. This period is marked by a profound conflict between the physical and the spiritual, particularly when aversion to bodily desires is most intense, coinciding with a time of vivid imagination and dreams. In contrast, girls experience an early sex drive that is not distinctly erotic. Instead, they may encounter unsettling longings, unfamiliar emotional stirrings, feelings of tenderness and gentle affection, and a yearning to love someone (Station, 1963).

Sexuality holds a significant role during adolescence, often intertwined with the concept of intimacy. Consequently, at this stage, both boys and girls who engage in romantic relationships are typically unable to experience mature love, often finding themselves in a state of infatuation.

Adolescent's Expression of Love

All typical expressions of heterosexual love serve to satisfy the ego. Each of these expressions provides the adolescent with a sense of security and addresses some of his primary needs, particularly his sexual needs, to a certain degree. At this stage, boys begin to experience new feelings towards specific girls. A girl captivates his thoughts; her slightest glance feels like paradise, he admires her handwriting, and her touch evokes a unique blend of pain and pleasure. He entertains dreams of protecting her, caring for her, and shielding her from harm. His feelings of love often manifest as a strange mix of tenderness and roughness, so when he kisses her, the gentleness can abruptly transform into intense excitement, which may intimidate the girl. However, such elements are essential in a man's love.

Anything that belongs to the beloved, especially if it has been chosen and utilized by her, is held in high regard due to its symbolic significance. He yearns for her constant presence and desires to share or communicate everything with her. Necking (a casual kiss above the neck) and petting (physical contact that stimulates erotic arousal without genital union) are prevalent in his relationships. When they are apart, the lover often writes love letters or poetry, or keeps a diary, makes calls or sends messages among other expressions of his feelings.

Walster assert that three conditions must be met for an individual to truly "fall in love": these include culture, the right partner, and a physiological arousal that is perceived as love. For numerous individuals, the distinction between love and infatuation becomes apparent only after a certain duration. If the feelings endure, it is deemed love; if the excitement diminishes swiftly, it is labelled infatuation. Plato posited that "falling in love" represents the earthly acknowledgment of souls that have been destined for one another in a prior celestial existence. Encountering the beloved is akin to a realization: "We loved before we were born."

Both men and women experience "falling in love" for a variety of reasons. When an individual observes someone possessing admirable qualities that they themselves lack, they may fall in love with the notion that their beloved will complete them. Additionally, "people often fall in love with their own romantic ideals rather than with a real human being" (due to the allure of an imagined hero or heroine). Consequently, disappointment arises when the true nature of their chosen partner begins to surface. At this juncture, they may either reject the beloved or attempt to mould them into their romantic ideals, which proves to be quite challenging.

The Theories of Romantic Attraction

There are numerous dimensions of romantic attraction as outlined below with various theories.

Persona Theory

The Persona theory posits that a significant element in the experience of falling in love or selecting a partner is how a prospective partner boosts one's self-esteem. Each individual possesses a mark, a persona, which represents the face presented to others. The persona theory indicates that individuals choose a partner who will enhance their self-image.

Imago Theory

Imago, derived from Latin meaning "image" refers to a composite representation of the individuals who have had the most profound influence during one's formative years. To a considerable extent, the romantic attraction one feels towards another person is depended upon how closely that individual matched with their imago.

John Robert Clark notes, "When the mental image one has of a loved one is influenced by childhood wishes, one may end up loving the image rather than the actual person behind it. Naturally, disappointment ensues if the person does not align with this image" (this is one of the reasons for breakups and divorces).

Need Gratification Theory

Henry A. Murray, Robert F. Winch, and their colleagues suggested that people who fall in love are often similar in social background but complementary in psychological needs. In choosing a partner, each person looks for someone who can best meet their needs. For example, a highly ambitious person may be drawn to a partner who enjoys supporting others. These needs can overlap, since a person can both want to help others and need help themselves.

Exchange Theory

Social psychologists introduced the concept of "Exchange Theory." The fundamental premise is that individuals tend to choose partners who are approximately their equals. Daniel Goleman, in the New York Times (July 22, 1982), reported on a study involving 537 dating men and women, revealing that those who viewed their partners as superior experienced feelings of guilt and insecurity. Conversely, individuals who perceived their partners as inferior reported feelings of anger. When partners regarded themselves as equals, their relationships tended to be relatively free of conflict and stable. Thus, it is not solely youth, beauty, and social status that attract individuals, but rather the entirety of the person, according to social psychologists.

Projected Image Theory

Carl Jung stated, "Every man carries his Eve in himself," suggesting that everyone holds a subconscious image of an ideal woman. Therefore, when a man and woman initially "fall in love," it is not with the true essence of the other person, but rather with a "projection" of what a beloved should embody. In this romantic relationship, a challenge arises as one may persistently cling to this image and attempt to mould the beloved to fit it, thereby remaining unaware of the beloved's true nature.

Evolutionary Theory of Sexual Attraction

The sexual impulse is inherently neutral, neither good nor evil, but rather a significant aspect of life that can lead to warmth and joy or to pain and destruction. Sexual attraction plays a crucial role in the journey of falling in love. This attraction originates in a small structure known as the hypothalamus, located deep within the primitive regions of the human brain.

Cultivating a Façade (illusion)

This refers to a psychological phenomenon of love termed "projective identification." In this process, an individual attempts to present themselves as more emotionally stable than they truly are. "After all, if he does not seem to have many personal needs, his partner is free to assume that his purpose in life is to nurture rather than to be nurtured." When this assumption proves incorrect, despair ensues in their relationship.

Anima-Animus Projection Theory

C.G. Jung observed that humans are "androgynous" a term derived from two Greek words meaning "man" and "woman." Thus, androgynous signifies that an individual's personality comprises both masculine (*animus*) and feminine (*anima*) traits. This notion is further supported by genetic science, which indicates that a man's sex is determined by possessing one more masculine gene than feminine, and conversely for women.

The Russian philosopher Nicholas Berdyaev stated, "man is not only a sexual but a bisexual being, combining the masculine and feminine principles within him in varying proportions and often in intense conflict. A man in whom the feminine principle was completely absent would be an abstract being… a woman lacking the masculine principle would not be a personality…. It is the union of these two principles that forms a complete human being." To achieve a fully alive or "individuated" (as termed by Jung) existence, there must be a balance between these elements.

A mature individual will exhibit equilibrium between anima and animus in both their conscious behaviours and unconscious psychological responses. Those lacking mature development will experience a strong attraction to individuals who outwardly display what is missing within their own character. "Friendships with individuals of the opposite sex, when managed appropriately, are among the most effective means to cultivate a proper balance between the anima and animus within one's personality."

Marie-Louise Von Franz once remarked that the anima represents "a personification of all feminine psychological tendencies within a man's psyche, such as vague feelings and moods." The male aspect or sexual function of the soul is accountable for order, logic, power, courage, and dependability, which are attributes of the intellect and will. Conversely, the female aspect interacts with matters of the heart, including the appreciation of art, music, religion, nature, and flowers.

Plutarch observed that the "soul of a lover resides in another's body." When a man projects an anima image onto a woman, she embodies his soul for him sexually, as if this connection would link him to his own soul. The man may believe he loves the woman profoundly, yet he remains unaware of the distinction between her true self and the anima image she represents for him. When this difference becomes clear, the fantasies he has constructed around her will disintegrate.

Mind in Attraction

The unconscious mind significantly influences mate selection. McClelland (1986) posits that an individual can articulate love or friendship as a logical process when engaging the left hemisphere of the brain, but the often-irrational experience of falling in love transpires only when the right hemisphere is activated.

Neuroscientist Paul McLean categorizes the brain into three concentric layers: *the brain stem,* which is the innermost and most primitive layer responsible for physical actions; *the limbic system,* which produces intense emotions; and *the cerebral cortex,* which houses the majority of cognitive functions. Harville Hendrix, a pastoral counsellor and therapist, merged the first two layers, referring to them as the 'old brain' (unconscious mind), while designating the third as the 'new brain' due to its more recent emergence in evolutionary history. The old brain appears to be concerned with categorizing individuals based on specific roles: whether to nurture, to be nurtured by, to engage in sexual relations with, to flee from, to submit to, or to attack. It processes images and compares them with previously stored memories, identifying them as 'this is my mother'; 'my cousin', 'my neighbour', 'my beloved'.

One's old brain, confined to the present moment and having only a faint awareness of the external world, is trying to recreate the childhood environment; this is driven by the necessity to heal past childhood traumas. Harville Hendrix states that "the fundamental reason for falling in love with another person is not merely that one's beloved is youthful and attractive, holds a prestigious job, possesses a comparable 'point value' or exhibits a kind nature. One falls in love because the old brain mistakenly associates the partner with one's parents! The old brain is convinced it has finally discovered the perfect candidate to compensate for the psychological and emotional harm endured during childhood. It believes that healing will occur through the simple act of merging with someone whom the old brain has misidentified as a caregiver, and who embodies the very aspects of the self that were suppressed in childhood". Furthermore, it is believed that one has rediscovered their lost self. As there is diminished desire for reciprocity, the focus shifts towards personal psychological and emotional development. Consequently, the likelihood of a breakup increases. Ultimately, losing that individual would equate to losing this newly formed sense of self.

The Hormones of Love

Psychopharmacological studies have revealed that individuals in love experience a natural high due to hormones and chemicals that flood their bodies, fostering a profound sense of well-being. During the attraction phase of a relationship, the brain releases dopamine and norepinephrine, two of the numerous neurotransmitters present in the body. These substances contribute to an optimistic perspective on life, an accelerated heart rate, heightened energy levels, and an enhanced sense of perception. They facilitate the experience of falling in love. When lovers are in each other's presence, the brain amplifies its production of endorphins and enkephalins, which are natural narcotics that bolster feelings of security and comfort. Dr. Michael R. Liebowitz posits that the increased production of serotonin engenders the mystical sensation of unity between lovers.

Helen Fisher, a scientist from the United States, has noted that the levels of dopamine and norepinephrine released by the brain tend to decline over time compared to the initial stages of love. This decline explains why lovers often remember and like the initial stage of their relationship, desiring their partner to embody the same qualities they exhibited at the beginning. However, vasopressin and oxytocin serve as the enduring protectors of love, being released during and after sexual intimacy. These hormones foster a commitment to the marital bond and the relationship. The precise triggers for the release of these powerful chemicals remain unclear, as does the reason for their reduction. In summary, romantic love constitutes an intense physical experience accompanied by quantifiable biological elements.

3

Process of Love

By the time most girls reach the ages of 12 or 13, and boys are around 13 or 14, they start to engage in romantic relationships. By the age of 16, over 90 percent of teenagers experience love for someone of the opposite sex or develop a profound affection. The experience of falling in love encompasses various levels, which ultimately lead to the ideal of human love.

Scanning

This initial stage occurs through eye contact. In this phase, the boy identifies the girl within the love framework he has constructed in his mind. If she aligns with his perception of love, attraction towards her begins to develop. Research by Exline and Winters (1965) indicates that women tend to gaze more at someone they like while conversing, whereas men are more likely to look when listening to someone they are fond of. Additionally, looking serves as a signal of sexual attraction during the scanning phase.

Attraction

At this stage, the boy experiences physical tension and excitement when he thinks about his beloved. He places greater emphasis on his appearance and becomes lost in thoughts of her. His mind is entirely consumed by her, and he feels a persistent desire to see and communicate with her. Consequently, he writes letters, makes phone calls, sends message and visits places she frequents, often as an unannounced guest. This sexual attraction can lead to infatuation.

Infatuation

Here, the lover's attention is directed towards the other individual, and everything appears to be positive. At this stage, rational thought is not engaged. There exists a principle of familiarity, where each person perceives their relationship as a continuation from a previous life. Additionally, there is a principle of discovery, wherein the boy identifies his beloved as an angel he has been searching for, while the girl believes she has found her Adam (or) Romeo. The principle of complementarity also arises, as one feels that their beloved completes the missing parts of themselves, leading to a sense of wholeness or perfection.

Disillusionment

As long as the lovers hold on to an idealized and incomplete perception of one another, they exist in a Garden of Eden. Following numerous encounters, they enter a close relationship characterized by excessive physical intimacy, even to the point of engaging in sexual intercourse. However, after the moment of realization, their infatuation begins to diminish. This marks the stage of disillusionment, during which they gradually start to take each other for granted, leading to a growing distance, minimal communication, and an overwhelming sense of resentment and hurt. Their needs and expectations remain unfulfilled, so their relationship becomes sour.

At this juncture, one's perception of their beloved becomes fragmented, leading to the belief that they have chosen the wrong partner. Hence, disappointment and despair ensue, culminating in a loss of love. If the lovers possess sufficient maturity, they will seek to understand where they went astray and seek to rediscover one another, choosing once more to love and prioritizing the relationship over individual desires and needs. In this way, the relationship can flourish anew. Those who continue to love despite disillusionment ultimately succeed in loving the beloved for who they truly are and come to understand the essence of love. Lederer and Jackson (1968) stated, "It is impossible to live in a permanent state of romance." Ordinary individuals should not feel frustrated or disheartened if they are not perpetually in a state of love.

4
Infatuation and Love

Love is not synonymous with infatuation; however, it cannot be entirely divorced from it either. Infatuation can manifest as a powerful physical sensation, which differs from 'love,' where mutual self-giving occurs. From a psychological perspective, infatuation and love represent two distinct yet interconnected stages of emotional attachment, each driven by different cognitive, emotional, and neurobiological processes. Understanding these differences helps explain why early romantic feelings appear intense and consuming, while mature love develops more gradually and endures over time.

Infatuation: An Intense Attraction

In the realm of relationships, infatuation is defined as a profound attraction to another individual, stemming from an intense focus on certain aspects of that person as if those features encapsulated their entirety. The term infatuation literally means "to be rendered foolish or lacking in sound judgment." Marie Mignon Mascaren characterizes it as a physical allure between two individuals of the opposite sex. J.R. Udry posits that infatuation is a term exclusively used to denote disapproval or a diminished love relationship.

Infatuation is typically the term employed when two adults experience a superficial and temporary love, often seen when middle-aged individuals unexpectedly fall for unusual partners. This state of infatuation is marked by fantasy and illusion, representing an immature, idealistic, and impractical view of love. Such a perspective dominates the individual's thoughts, striving to maintain this illusion. Ultimately, this romance is destined to encounter significant challenges, leading to heartbreak.

Infatuation is often the first phase of romantic involvement, especially common during adolescence and early relationships. Psychologically, it is characterized by idealization, where an individual focuses on a partner's positive traits while ignoring or minimizing flaws. Cognitive distortions such as *selective attention* and *fantasy projection* cause the person to imagine a perfect future, even with limited real knowledge of the other.

Emotionally, infatuation involves heightened excitement, obsession, and dependency. The individual may experience mood swings based on the partner's responses, approval, or availability. This phase is strongly influenced by dopamine, the brain's reward chemical, which creates feelings of pleasure, motivation, and craving. As a result, infatuation can feel addictive, leading to unwanted thoughts and a constant desire for emotional or physical closeness.

From a developmental standpoint, infatuation also plays a role in identity formation, particularly in teenagers. Romantic attention can temporarily boost self-esteem, but rejection or uncertainty may cause emotional distress, anxiety, or insecurity. Individuals with deeper emotional wounds tend to experience stronger infatuation. In reality, the girl serves merely as a catalyst in the boy's infatuation, with the underlying processes largely driven by hormones. Smart and Smart (1976) state, "Being in love is often temporary. The chemical arousal and the intense fixation on the object of one's affection are particularly floating during youth." There is no room for genuine love.

Love: The Deep Emotional Bonding

Love, in contrast, is a more stable and enduring emotional state that develops over time through shared experiences, trust, and mutual understanding. Psychologically, love involves realistic perception, where individuals acknowledge both strengths and weaknesses in their partner. Rather than fantasy-driven attachment, love is grounded in emotional intimacy, commitment, and empathy.

Neurobiologically, love is associated with chemicals such as **oxytocin and vasopressin**, which promote bonding, emotional security, and long-term attachment. These hormones support feelings of calmness, safety, and emotional closeness rather than the intense highs of infatuation.

Cognitively, love involves emotional regulation and adopting another's perspective. Individuals in love are better able to manage conflict, communicate openly, and prioritize mutual well-being. Love also supports psychological growth by fostering resilience, emotional maturity, and a sense of belonging.

Key Psychological Differences

a) Infatuation is driven by fantasy, novelty, and emotional dependency. Love is driven by reality, emotional security, and commitment.
b) Infatuation is intense but unstable; love is steady and enduring.
c) Infatuation centres on personal gratification; love emphasizes mutual care.

Psychologically, infatuation serves as the emotional spark that initiates romantic connection, while love represents its deeper, more meaningful evolution. Both play important roles in human development, but it is love that ultimately supports emotional stability, healthy relationships, and long-term psychological well-being.

Love at First Sight

This phenomenon represents a distinct category of infatuation. It embodies a potent emotion that propels an individual towards an object of affection that is unfamiliar to them. At first sight, the ecstasy of newfound love appears to emanate from the depths of the soul, from the eternal core of one's personality. However, its true origin is much lower. It primarily arises from instinct and the ego—two forces that, when poorly managed, can easily devolve into parasitic behaviours, ultimately becoming the sepulchre of the soul.

This love-at-first-sight experience is as authentic, sincere, and legitimate as puppy love (which transcends mere affection and involves minimal sexual elements), infatuation, which is predicated on the belief that one's deepest desires and needs can be satisfied by that other individual. Love at first sight is indeed feasible; one can, almost immediately upon introduction, be emotionally overwhelmed by another's allure. Here lies the prince or princess charming of one's dreams. This occurrence is frequent. However, the lovers will invariably possess years of personal growth behind them.

First Love

It encompasses more than mere sensuality and transience (existing for just a day). This is sufficiently demonstrated by all the loves that fade when the physical and romantic allure begins to diminish. Furthermore, while "first love may imprint itself in the blood with a dizzying effect, the love that lasts takes residence in the soul. In this manner, love transforms into something far more potent than mere flesh and bone. It provides the completeness necessary to navigate life safely."

Generally, first love manifests as a form of idolatry, not because of an excessive affection for the partner; rather, it is the opposite, as the only idol is the self. In this scenario, the object of a man's adoration is his own desire, the glorification of himself. The beloved's role is to serve as the source of the lover's pleasure. Consequently, they never truly engage with each other's essence; they never genuinely understand one another.

Love is an act of will, not merely a matter of sensibility or instinct that seeks its own gratification. As Nietzsche noted, lovers are not in love with their own inclination to love; what they initially love is the being to whom they incline. They appreciate the joy that arises from the being they love, yet that being is not incidental to their happiness: "I do not love you for what you provide; I love you for who you are." Thus, one should gradually cultivate greater mastery over instinct.

5
Romantic Love

One of the most profound human emotions is romantic love. It is often stated that "romantic love involves understanding the thoughts and feelings of one's partner and embracing them for who they truly are." Physical intimacy serves as a hallmark of a romantic relationship, distinguishing it from a close friendship. Intimacy can manifest in simple gestures such as kissing, holding hands, or embracing, but it may also encompass a range of sexual activities. The essence of intimacy is influenced by factors such as physical closeness, eye contact, facial expressions (like smiling), the nature of the conversation (how personal it is), and the tone of voice (which should be warm), etc.

The typical romantic lover aspires to achieve a complete emotional connection with the partner. The flames of this love style are largely ignited by a strong sense of physical attraction. There exists a compelling urgency to unite both physically and emotionally. A romantic lover does not demand love but is instead ready to embrace it when it appears. Most individuals agree that a significant physical attraction exists between lovers, particularly in the initial phases of their relationship.

This attraction is frequently accompanied by various physiological responses, including accelerated breathing, heightened pulse rate, and muscle tension. In other words, the individual "in love" experiences a general emotional arousal when contemplating the beloved or when in their presence. Naturally, such a response could merely indicate sexual attraction rather than true "love." However, if this physical attraction is coupled with a strong and deepening emotional bond, along with a pronounced tendency to idealize and obsess over the person, then these reactions are more indicative of genuine love.

Love Styles in Romantic Relationships

According to Hendrick and Hendrick (1986), there are six distinct love styles in romantic relationships, which are outlined as follows.

Eros

This style is referred to as passionate love. It represents an immediate and intense attraction to the physical appearance of the beloved. While contemporary usage often confines the term 'erotic' to sexual connotations, Eros transcends mere sexual fascination; it embodies a fervent quest for the lover's ideal of beauty. The erotic lover's reliance on an idealized concept of beauty frequently results in disappointment. These individuals often experience 'love at first sight'; however, such love is seldom lasting.

Ludus

This style is characterized by game-playing love. The motto of the ludic lover is, "love multiple individuals, as three lovers are safer than two, and two are much safer than one." He tends to avoid intimacy with the beloved and will not permit the partner to become overly attached to him. He embodies a cynical player; when he is not in proximity to the girl he loves, he finds affection for the girl who is nearby.

Storge

This love is rooted in deep friendship, rather than being a mysterious or mystical emotion; it is a calm and enchanting affection. Storge represents a slow-burning love, where one does not abruptly fall in love but gradually wanders into the realm of love. He will not hold hatred for someone he once loved. While there is an absence of ecstasy, there is also a lack of despair.

Mania

It literally signifies madness. It represents a possessive form of love where the lover cannot endure their beloved's connections with others, leading to intense jealousy. The lover is overwhelmed by thoughts of the beloved. Symptoms such as agitation, insomnia, fever, loss of appetite, and heartache accompany this state. Fuelled by popular media, mania has become increasingly prevalent among the youth. However, this type of love does not mature; instead, it often ends prematurely.

Pragma

This type of love is characterized by logic, where the beloved's similar background holds significant importance. Pragma emphasizes compatibility based on practical criteria, where compatible personalities, shared interests, education, and other factors play a crucial role.

Agape

Agape is a selfless form of love in which one is willing to sacrifice their life for the beloved. It embodies altruistic and universal love that is consistently kind and patient, devoid of jealousy and demands for reciprocity. Agape, in its purest form, is seldom found among lovers.

In the romantic relationships of young individuals, research has shown that among these six love styles, storge (friendship love) is the most popular, followed by Eros (passionate love).

Four Phenomena of Romantic Love

Harville Hendrix, after analysing the lovers, reduced romantic love into four fundamental statements.

1. During the initial or second meeting, the first statement manifests as follows: "I know we've just met, but somehow I feel as though I already know you." He referred to this as

the *'**Phenomenon of recognition,**'* where lovers perceive a sense of familiarity, as if they have known each other for years. This feeling of familiarity suggests that they have unconsciously rediscovered their caretakers.

2. A few weeks later, the second statement arises: "This is peculiar, but even though we've only been seeing each other for a short time, I can't remember when I didn't know you." This is termed the *'**Phenomenon of timelessness,**'* which evokes a sense of togetherness that transcends temporal limitations.
3. Subsequently, at a more mature stage, the third statement emerges: "When I'm with you, I no longer feel alone; I feel whole, complete." This is known as the *'**Phenomenon of reunification,**'* stemming from an individual's ongoing quest for completeness.
4. Finally, lovers express their ultimate declaration of love: "I love you so much, I can't live without you." This represents the *'**Phenomenon of necessity,**'* where they become intertwined in such a way that they cannot imagine a separate existence. They emulate the bond between mothers and their new-born, cherishing and delighting in every aspect of each other's beings. They vow to love each other in a manner that surpasses any love previously experienced.

Steinberg's Triangular Theory of Love

Steinberg does not favour the classification of love into companionate love and passionate love; instead, he proposed the Triangular Theory, which aids in distinguishing between infatuation and love. He posits that love consists of three primary components: ***intimacy, passion,*** *and* ***commitment***. Based on the dominant component in a specific relationship, he categorizes the various types of love.

1. Intimacy serves as an emotional component, encompassing feelings of closeness and connectedness. It also includes elements such as affection, communication, support, and sharing.
2. Passion involves the motivational drives associated with sex, physical closeness, and romance. This component is characterized by intense, physiologically arousing feelings of attraction, marked by physical arousal and a strong desire to be with the loved one.
3. Decision/Commitment represents both the initial recognition of love for another person and the long-term resolve to sustain that love.

According to Steinberg's theory of love, these three distinct components of love fluctuate in their influence over time and follow distinct courses. In strong loving relationships, for example, the level of commitment reaches a peak and then stabilizes, while intimacy continues to develop throughout the relationship. Passion tends to increase rapidly in the early stages of a relationship but gradually declines over time, although it remains a significant component of loving relationships.

The Combinations of love

	Components		
	Intimacy	Passion	Decision / Commitment
Non love	-	-	-
Liking	+	-	-
Infatuated Love	-	+	-
Empty Love	-	-	+
Romantic love	+	+	-
Companionate Love	+	-	+
Fatuous Love	-	+	+
Consummate Love	+	+	+

(+ = Component present; - = Component absent)

Given that all three components are crucial for a loving relationship, it is incorrect to regard consummate love as the "ideal" form of love, because Numerous long - lasting and completely satisfactory relationships are based on types of love that differ from consummate love. Furthermore, the dominant type of love within a relationship can shift over time. Steinberg's triangular theory of love highlights the intricate nature of love and its dynamic, evolving characteristics. As individuals and their relationships grow and transform, so too does their love.

The Expectations of Men and Women in Love

The criteria for falling in love vary between men and women. What attracts an individual to a friend is based on what he knows about him; in a woman it is what he doesn't know. This is why friendships often deepen as one explores the inner self of a friend, while love, as noted by Proust, can diminish when a woman's mystery is unveiled. A man loves a woman for her attributes; for him, loving a woman equates to prefer her. Thus, he has, or thinks he has, reasons for loving her. It is often said that a woman is more 'blind' in love than a man, as her feelings are less anchored in rationality.

Women's love is less influenced by intellect compared to men. They love men for who they are and often confused love with the reasons for loving. 'A woman can be in love with someone and filled with admiration for him, yet remain fully aware of all his flaws.' Therefore, a man can fully disclose his true self to her, including his most undesirable traits, without jeopardizing her affection. However, to gain or maintain the love of the one he adores, men tend to conceal their own imperfections and misdeeds, which proves to be an impossible task.

Men are inspired to engage in romantic relationships through visual stimuli, whereas women are ignited by a man's verbal expressions of affection. Oscar Wilde echoes this sentiment through his female character who states, "We women, as someone says, love with our ears, just as you men love with your eyes, if you ever even love at all." From an evolutionary perspective, it is suggested that "men are attracted to classically beautiful women—those with clear skin, bright eyes, lustrous hair, well-defined bone structure, red lips, and rosy cheeks—not due to trends or fashion, but because these traits signify youth and robust health, indicators that a woman is at the peak of her childbearing years."

Men prioritize physically appealing, younger women as they are more capable of bearing children over an extended period. "Since youth and physical health are not critical to the male reproductive role, women instinctively prefer partners with pronounced 'alpha' traits, the ability to dominate other males and bring home more than their fair share of the skill."

Women are inclined to choose partners who can offer resources that benefit their children. As a result, they are drawn to partners who present the greatest potential for economic stability. This explains why contemporary young women often find themselves attracted to individuals with possessions or wealthy backgrounds, often placing less emphasis on character.

Research conducted by Rubin & Hill (1981) indicates that men tend to fall in love more readily than women, while women are more likely to fall out of love more easily than men. On the contrary, for a woman in love, a man represents an end goal, whereas for a man, she is often viewed as a means to an end or a combination of both, even if he holds deep affection for her. A man desires, while a woman gives, and she expects from him not a love devoid of desire, but rather a steadfastness in his longing for her. She wishes for the happiness of her beloved, but that happiness must originate solely from her. Within her lies a form of greedy and exclusive altruism that has to be purified.

The question arises: are women truly complicated? The answer is a resounding no! Women are fundamentally simple, transparent, and easy to comprehend. The perceived complexity attributed to women stems from a man's failure to recognize their inherent simplicity.

Part Five
Challenges and Solutions

Love often begins with idealized expectations of happiness and fulfilment, yet it frequently presents challenges that test emotional maturity and understanding. Individuals, especially in early romantic experiences, may encounter frustration when expectations are unmet, anxiety arising from uncertainty, and fear of losing personal independence. Feelings of jealousy, possessiveness, and the pain of relationship failure further complicate the experience of love. In contemporary society, love is sometimes misunderstood or reduced to physical intimacy, leading to confusion and emotional distress. The following pages examine common issues encountered in love relationships and explores constructive approaches, the characteristics of genuine love, and pathways toward emotional healing and growth.

1
Love and Sex

Falling in love is fundamentally an erotic experience linked to sex, which is often misinterpreted as love. One truly falls in love only when there is a conscious or unconscious sexual motivation involved. Paul Geraldy has articulated that the skin-deep affection, often mistaken for love by many in modern society, is merely a sexual inclination. Sex represents the most profound, affectionate, and loving act, transcending mere physicality to embody spiritual communication. It becomes distorted and unattractive when misused in the absence of love. Those who perceive sex solely as a source of pleasure tend to view their beloved as an object—something to be utilized for gratification—thereby missing the essence of love. They may employ love as a means to attain sex, whereas a mature individual experiences love, with sex naturally serving as a means of expressing that love. Sex is regarded as a form of body language, characterized primarily by genital penetration, which ultimately provides exquisite pleasure. However, this pleasure reveals nothing about the individual behind it.

Etymology of Sex and Its Implications

The term 'sex' originates from the Latin verb '*secare*', which translates to "to cut". This suggests that God, having created human nature, divided it into two parts: male and female. The entire personality theory surrounding heterosexuality indicates that neither half can exist without being connected to the other half. In Plato's Symposium, Aristo Phanes perceives sex as a reunion with the other half of one's self.

This concept is echoed in the Upanishads, which describe the creation of man: "But he felt no delight; thus, a man who is alone experiences no joy." Consequently, a wife was created to fill this emptiness. This perspective aligns closely with the Biblical account of Adam and Eve. Both Alfred North Whitehead and Paul Tillich maintained that reality possesses an ontological nature characterized by negative-positive polarity, meaning that all of reality embodies a male-female essence. Paul Tillich, who identifies Hegel as a Philosopher of Love, remarked that "Hegel's dialectical framework is an abstraction derived from his concrete understanding of love as both separation and reunion."

Sexual Love

Sexual love manifests on two distinct levels. The first level encompasses profound feelings of tenderness, admiration, and aesthetic appreciation, while the second level involves a strong desire for tactile and typically genital contact. This form of love is nourished by instinct and the ego, two forces that fundamentally oppose any form of communion and emotional openness. Consequently, this type of love remains fundamentally subjective. It is characterized by persistent irritability, a sense of suspicion, conflict, and jealousy.

In sexual love, individuals are physically present with one another, yet only the physical aspect of the other is acknowledged; they merely coexist. Thus, it is essential to engage with one another to foster reciprocal love. Girls often derive joy from the sensations associated with hugging and kissing, whereas boys may view such pleasures merely as a means to an end. For girls, sexual feelings are intricately linked to feelings of love; conversely, for boys, initial sexual impulses tend to be quite distinct from such emotions. Ultimately, love is an act of will rather than a matter of sensibility, which is often regarded as an adversary to love.

The Essence of Love Encompasses Both Body and Soul

The paradox inherent in love lies within the interplay of body and soul; the source of all conflicts and calamities in love stems from these contrasts. However, the strength of love serves to harmonize these differences. This does not imply that the physical aspect should be disregarded in a loving relationship, but rather that it should be managed to prevent it from overshadowing the soul. Nietzsche may aptly provide the concluding thought: "In true love, it is the soul that envelops the body."

Human love represents a union of body and spirit between individuals. Initially, the physical aspect of love tends to dominate, but as love matures, a balance is achieved between body and spirit. In the fully developed stage of love, the spiritual aspect is prioritized. If one is not entirely uplifted by sexual love, they may find themselves diminished by it. Genuine love between a man and a woman does not commence in the physical realm and conclude in the spiritual; rather, there exists an unavoidable blending of soul and body from its inception to its culmination. In love, true joy is not that which descends from the lips to the heart, but rather that which rises from the heart to the lips. If affection is solely directed towards the physical form of the beloved, it is not love but mere lust.

Love and Premarital Sex

The yearning for sexual connection intensifies as love deepens. Initially, love seeks proximity to the beloved. Both individuals increasingly express their affection and soon desire to manifest their love through the complete intimacy of the sexual act. This appears to be the ultimate demonstration of love, seeking no boundaries and focusing solely on the present pleasure, where they overlook potential repercussions. They rationalize their actions by claiming that certain circumstances may delay or obstruct their marriage, thus they do not wish to forgo the sexual aspect of a loving relationship. Additionally, some engage in premarital sex before concluding their love affair, asserting that they are making a selfless sacrifice for their partner. However, the reality is that for them, a love centered on sexuality is essential. Consequently, this behavior leads to feelings of guilt, making it difficult for them to confront each other in the future.

Premarital Sex and Disillusionment

Premarital sex serves as a gateway through which disillusionment can infiltrate the soul, diminishing the charms of a loved one and shifting focus on the imperfections and shortcomings within the romantic relationship. The disillusioned partner, who believes they have fully explored the object of their affection, has merely skimmed the surface of that love. In reality, they face their own limitations and lack of control. What they admired in the other is, in essence, a reflection of themselves. Disillusionment arises from the conflict of the ego with itself. During this crisis, one may become harsh and unkind towards their beloved.

Dr. Beverley Mead (Psychiatrist) posits that sexual activity should encompass love, a sense of belonging, and a lasting relationship - elements often absent in many premarital sexual encounters. While excitement and desire may be present, they are frequently accompanied by anxiety, concerns about potential repercussions, guilt, and disappointment regarding the overall situation. Consequently, this leads to frustration and uncertainty about whether a couple is personally and sexually compatible. If the initial sexual experience is enjoyable, fulfilling, or reassuring, and is not followed by disappointment or disillusionment, subsequent similar experiences are likely to remain equally pleasant and satisfying. When the body and heart signal a 'no' but the mind compels a 'yes,' the resulting damage to the psyche can endure into adulthood, transforming sex into a joyless experience. The disappointment or disillusionment stemming from negative experiences with premarital sex can significantly impact an individual's post-marriage sexual life.

In moments of disillusionment, individuals often blame one another for the suffering and disappointments that stem from the collapse of their love. At this stage, one exhibits ingratitude not only towards the beloved but also towards love itself. Although love persists despite disillusionment, lovers may encounter a form of 'unexplained hatred' due to the feeling that they have tarnished their love with the fleeting pleasures of the flesh, which was once a genuine and sacred bond. Furthermore, the continuation of a romantic relationship may represent an artificial compromise between two souls driven by the need for external passions. During these dry spells, lovers tend to return to the cradle of their affection, often saying, 'Do you remember how our love started?' They yearn for the emotions of the past and wish to see their partner as they were in the beginning.

One must not cling to past dreams; these must be allowed to fade away. Those who genuinely continue to love despite disillusionment ultimately succeed in loving the beloved for who they truly are, leading to a state of self-surrender. They become capable of connecting with the soul of their beloved, and their love transforms into something pure and tender, devoid of any expectation of reciprocity from the beloved.

Psychological counseling suggests that premarital sex, despite initial pleasure, tends to become increasingly less meaningful and fulfilling. This decline in instinct leads to suspicions, jealousy, misunderstandings, lovers' quarrels, and fluctuations between extreme joy and deep despair. Therefore, sexual intercourse should be regarded as a privilege reserved for married individuals, as it represents a complete expression of love and dependency—elements that cannot realistically exist without the assurance of a permanent and binding marriage commitment. Thus, it should not be considered an appropriate method for assessing the authenticity of a romantic relationship.

Adolescent Love and Sexuality

Among certain teenagers and young adults, there exists a desire to assert their masculinity. Consequently, various forms of sexual intimacy, such as deep kissing, necking, petting, massaging, oral sex, and ultimately sexual intercourse, manifest within adolescent relationships. According to Dr. Mead, boys often do not experience disappointment with premarital sex unless it conflicts with their moral values. Conversely, girls are significantly more likely to feel disappointed. This is because, for them, sex is intertwined with love, and their romantic notions of the experience being wonderful, tender, and exciting are frequently unmet in premarital encounters. As a result, they may feel cheated or used, especially if the boy does not develop a deeper romantic inclination towards them after the experience, which is often the case.

In the context of premarital sex, a girl who gives herself, even under unlawful circumstances, may experience a sense of well-being or the 'good conscience' of fulfilling her purpose and realizing her destiny. For her, the act of offering herself represents the ultimate reality that justifies and explains all her love. In contrast, the boy in love is never completely satisfied with himself; he perpetually seeks reasons to justify his passion. Through sexual intimacy, the girl who presents herself as a gift envisions the beloved's acceptance and a profound emotional connection. However, the boy, who pursues selfish pleasure and readily accepts such a gift, is inherently incapable of forming deep attachments or exhibiting fidelity.

A nationwide survey conducted in the U.S.A in 1970, which interviewed 400 young individuals aged 13 to 19, revealed that 59 percent of boys and 45 percent of girls reported having engaged in sexual intercourse at least once. Additionally, a survey conducted in Mumbai in 2005 by Time (Mumbai Mirror), a leading magazine in Asia, indicates that 58 percent of college students in Mumbai have had pre-marital sex. Furthermore, the age at which adolescents first engage in sexual intercourse has been consistently declining. In the U.S.A, half of adolescents experience sexual intercourse between the ages of 15 and 18, and at least 80 percent have had sexual relations before reaching the age of 20 (Seidman and Reider, 1994). If so, think about the present situation.

Permissiveness with Affection

According to the newly established norm known as 'permissiveness with affection' in Western nations, premarital sex is considered as acceptable for both genders, provided it occurs within the framework of a long-term, committed, or loving relationship. Men and women exhibit differing responses to the inquiry, "How long should one be acquainted with a person before engaging in sexual activity? For one hour? One day?" (And so forth, extending up to five years). While both genders are more likely to affirm this as the duration of their romantic relationship lengthens, men tend to be more willing than women to consent to sexual relations at all the levels up to two years. However, once the acquaintance has lasted for five years, the gender disparity diminishes, meaning that both men and women are in agreement regarding sexual relations (within a loving relationship) after knowing someone for approximately five years.

Romantic Involvement with A Married Individual (an older person)

Teenage girls perceive a married man as experienced and mature. Girls tend to mature faster than boys of the same age, leading them to view boys as childish and foolish, while they fantasize about the charms of older men (such as a teacher, a friend's brother, or friends of their father). For these girls, married men appear to be safe, and the fact that he is married offers a sense of protection. His marital status suggests that he has had the opportunity to learn how to give and receive affection in a manner that resonates with a woman's needs and feelings. Consequently, girls often regard him as lovable.

However, married men may also be emotionally unfulfilled; for instance, a misunderstood husband might seek solace in other girls by talking about how his wife fails to understand him, thereby eliciting sympathy from them. In turn, she may attempt to compensate for his wife's shortcomings through her attention and care. "Once a man has experienced the fullness of a woman's love, he learns to expect it and feels entitled to it perpetually."

The same dynamics apply to teenage boys, who find married women appealing. A married woman has demonstrated her desirability to at least one man who chose to marry her. Teenage boys often find their affections directed towards someone reminiscent of their mother, as a married woman may evoke maternal qualities. A lonely and emotionally starved married woman has easy access to men and boys of various backgrounds. This interaction may begin with simple encounters and can quickly envelop the boy. Conversely, a mature woman who is content with her own marriage is less likely to succumb to such temptations. Instead, she may assist the boy in a nurturing manner, helping him to move beyond his infatuation. She calls for the same loyalty that he has offered to his mother.

Developing romantic feelings for a married individual is generally considered inappropriate. However, this situation is not particularly rare. Young women who experienced a lack of paternal attention during their formative years often derive a unique sense of fulfillment from the interest shown by older men, while young men who lacked maternal affection may seek out relationships with older women. Consequently, it can be said that girls are more likely to become involved in relationships with older individuals than boys. Fortunately, the majority of both girls and boys tend to move past this phase quite rapidly and may later reflect on these early infatuations with a sense of amused nostalgia.

Sex Education and Love

Sex education is not limited to learning a set of do's and don'ts; many individuals may know these facts yet still fail to understand the true essence of sexuality. This shortcoming stems from a deficiency in love. No amount of sexual knowledge can compensate for an absence of love. The primary aim of sex education is to assist individuals in understanding themselves as human beings and to value the dignity inherent in human love. Consequently, it fosters the development of loving and responsible individuals.

Parents Serve as Educators Regarding Sexuality

In his article titled "Parents are sex educators, whether they know it or not," Vivian Ziegler asserts that "if parents embrace their own sexuality and find joy in expressing love to their partners, they actively provide sex education to their children." Dr. H. Clair Amstutz, in his book "Growing up to Love," states, "when a child is old enough to ask a specific question, he has already demonstrated his ability to comprehend a direct answer." Consequently, when a child inquires about sex, parents can offer honest and direct answers that are appropriate to the child's age. Additionally, Weininger notes, "If teenagers do not feel love from their parents, they may perceive sex as a means to obtain it." Thus, parental love is crucial for the healthy sexual development of their children.

2
Possessive Love

Jealous love can be described as a possessive form of affection, where one clings to their partner, believing that they belong solely to them. This type of love is arguably the most unfulfilling and troubling style of love. It shifts between excitement and strong desire, and can quickly turn from devotion to jealousy. This occurs because individuals who are obsessively preoccupied with the well-being of their partner often develop issues related to possessiveness and jealousy.

Characteristics of Possessive Love

In possessive love, there exists a persistent and profound yearning to completely own the beloved, while simultaneously desiring to be owned by them. This dynamic is accompanied by an ever-present fear of loss or rejection. From these lovers, two conflicting emotional elements can be observed: they exhibit significant dependency and struggle to manage their intense emotional responses. Conversely, they tend to be demanding, often imposing considerable emotional strain on their partner, are highly sensitive, and remain vigilant for any indication that their partner's affection appears to be diminishing. Furthermore, it is important to note that excessive possessiveness can lead to jealousy, ultimately resulting in bitterness.

Jealousy in Love

The modern philosopher René Descartes characterizes jealousy as a form of fear associated with the desire to retain a certain possession. Furthermore, to assert that love is devoid of jealousy seems evidently incorrect, as jealousy serves as a motivating force that drives an individual to seek the utmost pleasure and goodness. When one observes that another possesses more, there arises a desire for more as well. However, this desire does not stem from a wish to deprive the beloved of their possessions; rather, it is a longing to share in those joys. In essence, the desire for increased pleasure and goodness is not inherently negative, but when it escalates to an excessive level, it can consume the individual and foster resentment, potentially leading them to irrationally distance themselves from their beloved.

Jealousy embodies a type of fear—the fear of losing someone—and it also manifests as a form of pain—the pain of being excluded from the life of the loved one. Jealousy is a painful emotion stemming from the fear of losing connection with the beloved, particularly when they seem to be taken away by another.

According to Jersild (1954), jealousy is perceived as a blend of emotions including anxiety, grief, anger, self-pity, dejection, fear, and hostility, rather than being a singular, primary emotion. When an individual feels secure within themselves, they do not perceive others as a threat; however, if they feel insecure, they become envious of others. They lack a sense of worth. When uncertain about their own value, they are perpetually haunted by the fear that someone more worthy will come along and take away their beloved. Even a simple smile directed at their partner or a casual greeting can be perceived as a threat.

A minor negative attitude, a small lie, or a slight indifference from their beloved can instill in them a persistent anxiety that they may be rejected at any moment. This situation also fosters doubt regarding their security and undermines their self-esteem. Such feelings can lead to anger and guilt, resulting in a life filled with confusion between uncertainty and self-rejection. Jealousy grows stronger when the person has nothing in life except their partner. The person who expresses the sentiment, "I can't live without you," is confronting a profound threat to their very identity when faced with the possibility of losing the one they cannot imagine living without. This individual is perpetually on guard against the worst outcomes, and this very suspicion can provoke harsh reactions.

Sexual Jealousy and Aggression

Since erotic love arises from a sense of need, the erotic lover desires the beloved to dedicate her entire self exclusively to him. When he perceives that someone or something is encroaching upon her life, he experiences the anguish of loss. This anguish manifests as jealousy. It is commonly understood that sexual jealousy involves the perception of a threat to a romantic relationship posed by a competitor for one's partner. This feeling can serve as a significant catalyst for aggression. Individuals who believe their partner has wronged them by engaging in flirtation with another person frequently encounter intense feelings of anger and may often contemplate or engage in actions aimed at punishing their partner, the rival, or both, typically directing their anger more towards the beloved than the rival.

Transcending Jealous Love

Jealousy appears to be an ever-present aspect of love. It is born from love and sustained by it. When love fades, jealousy also perishes. Consequently, an erotic lover must be prepared to endure the anguish of jealousy to fully appreciate the pleasures of love. People require both separation and independence from their partners as much as they desire closeness with them. However, erotic love insists on complete possession and seeks to be integrated into the other person's plans, aiming for total fulfillment through another individual. Such expectations, however, are inherently unattainable. Love is the ability to feel joy when your beloved has experiences that don't include you. This kind of love rises above jealousy and overcomes fear, even the fear of loss. Studies on sexual jealousy indicate that when someone else is involved in the life of the beloved, women tend to experience more intense feelings of jealousy and anger towards both their partner and the rival compared to men.

3
Understanding Love: Elements That Matter

Love is often spoken of as a feeling that happens naturally, yet sustaining a genuine love relationship requires far more than emotion alone. It is a complex interplay of understanding, commitment, communication, trust, and emotional maturity. While attraction may spark a love affair, it is awareness of these deeper elements that allows love to grow, endure, and transform over time. Understanding love is not merely about knowing how to feel, but about learning how to relate, respond, and evolve with another person. The essential factors that shape a healthy and meaningful love relationship are explained here. By becoming aware of the following elements, individuals can move beyond idealized notions of love and develop relationships grounded in authenticity and emotional balance.

Attention and Intention

For those who experience love, the attention given tends to decrease as the number of loved ones increases; however, this does not necessarily diminish the strength of intention. Attention is associated with the mind, which consistently focuses on the loved one, allowing the lover to be vividly aware of her presence and actions. Conversely, intention pertains to the will, representing the will in action. The will aims to direct both the mind and senses towards the beloved. While the mind may operate in a singular direction, the will can navigate multiple paths. Therefore, when the mind is preoccupied with other matters (where the beloved is not actively considered at that moment), the will remains connected to the loved one.

The will maintains a continuous link with the beloved and redirects the mind's attention as soon as it chooses to focus in that direction. She becomes an integral part of his very existence, even when absent from physical perception. Both are present in each other's minds and wills, perpetually thinking of one another. If the beloved occupies a place in one's will, nothing can displace them. Thus, a clear understanding of the dynamics of attention and intention in love can help in alleviating feelings of possessiveness and jealousy.

Self-Doubt

True love includes understanding and accepting yourself—both strengths and flaws—because someone who can't face their own faults is unlikely to accept those of others. Such a person may hold negative feelings about themselves, which in turn leads to negative feelings towards everyone around them. "Doubt yourself and you doubt the world." This form of self-doubt can poison all relationships. Conversely, if a person is self-fulfilled, they can even come to terms with the experience of their beloved departing, if that is the path necessary for their beloved's own fulfillment.

Transference or Mistaken Identity

The psychological concept known as "Transference" refers to the phenomenon of attributing the characteristics of one individual to another. Individuals in romantic relationships often project their emotions regarding their parents onto their partners, as they have, through an unconscious selection process, chosen partners who bear a resemblance to their parents or caregivers. Even if the person identified is incorrect, it can be challenging to cut off that connection, and they may even refuse to acknowledge the pain inflicted by that partner. This is because that individual serves as a means to fulfill one's unconscious childhood desires.

Pitying

Pitying refers to the act of 'feeling sorry'. It often gets confused with love itself. One of the simplest ways to draw attention and care is to appeal to another's sympathies. In this scenario, an individual expresses, "How can you be so cruel? I am so weak that if you do not meet my expectations, I will be devastated." In this state, one tends to empathize with the other and feels pity for her. If this emotion manifests as a form of possession, it will persist until the needs of the other are fulfilled. That may never happen, because once the care stops, her suffering returns. Consequently, withdrawing one's feelings appears to be an act of unforgivable cruelty. Thus, one becomes ensnared. There is no way out without causing harm to someone.

Feeling sorry for someone is not love; it is a kind of forced affection. It prevents real love from growing and is exhausting for everyone involved. Essentially, individuals who exploit another's sympathies possess a sense of self-pity. This originates from their focus on their own painful experiences, leading to a list of grievances such as, "Nobody loves me, nobody understands me, I have endured a difficult life, I am perpetually suffering, there is no hope for me." In their own mental court, they rationalize their self-pity. Consequently, they seek the sympathy of others, while those who feel pity for others attempt to place themselves in their position. They imagine what others are feeling based on their own experiences and sensitivities. "To over indulge in pitying other can hinder the self-confidence of the other in overcoming the sufferings"

Sacrifice in Love

The readiness to make sacrifices for another person signifies love and reflects an abundance of affection. However, this is not always the case, as there may be unworthy motivations behind such sacrifices. Three of these motivations are outlined here.

Possessiveness; "a person who desires to possess another is capable of making significant sacrifices. Indeed, the larger the sacrifice made for someone else, the greater the debt incurred." Such sacrifices result in enslavement rather than love. *Image;* an individual who presents an image of perfection to conceal their flaws and fears of rejection is also capable of making sacrifices. These sacrifices are for appearances, not for love. *Guilt;* "a person who feels guilty towards another can make substantial sacrifices to alleviate the persistent discomfort they experience." Even if the sacrifice is driven by sincere reasons, it does not equate to love itself, but rather stems from love.

Expectation In Love

There is nothing inherently wrong with a lover who expects reciprocation of affection from their beloved. However, excessive expectation can lead to dissatisfaction. When one expects more from another than they are capable of providing, it often results in a rupture of the relationship and a need to forget. Therefore, an individual who values their partner is unlikely to demand more expressions of love than what she is willing to offer.

In romantic relationships, someone may expect their partner to meet all their needs and see it as proof of love. If she doesn't, she may be called a "bad" partner, even though no one can realistically satisfy all of another person's needs. Such expectations can damage a loving relationship, as the unfulfilled partner may blame their beloved. This, in turn, causes feelings of unfairness, defensiveness, and inferiority, leading to misunderstandings. This pattern of expectation is prevalent among possessive lovers and can ultimately result in the dissolution of their love.

Freedom and Love

Freedom represents the absence of any constraints, yet it must be guided by a purpose. An individual's freedom does not consist in doing anything and behaving as he wishes because it is not mere randomness but must be exercised rationally and responsibly. This is why Sartre asserts, "Man is condemned to freedom." Conversely, St. Augustine was wary of excessive freedom, as he believed it could lead to sin.

Anyone who loves should acknowledge that they are losing fifty percent of their independence. This process should occur spontaneously and naturally, driven by love rather than compulsion. For instance, in a romantic relationship, when a girl agrees to be with a boy, she sacrifices her freedom in the name of love, which means she can no longer spend time with other boys. She must dedicate less time to her friends, placing them in a secondary position in her life; her beloved now occupies the primary role, and she must be mindful of her actions to ensure he does not feel hurt or leave her for any reason.

Freedom in love signifies the ability to be attracted to one another in mutual affection while maintaining one's individual identity, free from being imprisoned by another's thoughts, words, and actions. One must honor the freedom of their beloved, and both individuals should exercise their freedom with certain limitations to ensure the harmonious operation of their romantic relationship.

Love does not cancel anyone's rights. Agapic love means choosing to give up what you are entitled to, freely and willingly. If the lovers do not experience agapic love, there will be ongoing disputes concerning their freedom. One partner may insist on their freedom while the other may vehemently resist it. The individual who fails to respect their beloved's freedom exhibits arrogance or rudeness. Arrogance comes from trying to gain power when feeling insecure, while rudeness puts others down to feel superior. By denying the beloved's freedom, one seeks reassurance, support, and respect, which is ultimately unattainable.

The willingness of a person to risk everything for their beloved's freedom is invariably accompanied by suffering. The pain intensifies when the beloved utilizes the freedom granted to distance themselves from the lover for the sake of another individual. This notion aligns with Sartre's perspective on human love. He posits that in human love, the lover seeks to possess the freedom of the beloved. "It is the possession of the beloved's freedom as freedom." Even if the lover and beloved succeed in forming a lasting bond, the presence of a 'third' party (the Other) renders it a dead possibility. Thus, Sartre asserts, "Hell is the other," as the lover's subjectivity is threatened by the third individual. True love cannot flourish in the presence of another. This futile pursuit culminates in 'Masochism' and 'Sadism'.

Dependency

Scott Pect characterizes dependency as "The inability to experience wholeness or to function adequately without the assurance that one is being actively cared for by another." In physically healthy adults, dependency is considered pathological; it is a risk and often a manifestation of a mental illness or defect. This form of dependency is passive, stemming from an inner sense of emptiness. Furthermore, it directly results from a parent's failure to meet their child's needs for affection, attention, and care during formative years. Such individuals become so preoccupied with seeking love that they lack the energy to give love in return. Conversely, mutual dependence is a natural state that reflects integrity and is associated with unconditional love.

Two Types of Dependence

The first type involves relying on one's partner for physical, social, and emotional support. However, if this support is unexpectedly removed or unavailable, a mature and authentic individual does not fall apart. They are capable of temporarily living without their loved one.

The second type of dependency appears similar on the surface, but if the support is withdrawn, that individual experiences a collapse. Such a person lacks freedom in their love, which is conditioned by their fear of losing the one they are entirely dependent on.

Independence

Independence is discovered when a lover can fully support the beloved's balanced growth in personality while simultaneously allowing the beloved's complete freedom to evolve in their own distinct manner. In this form of love, there are no conditions or demands; it embodies a profound trust in the goodness of the other as a response. In reciprocal love, where dependency is emphasized, both individuals often experience discomfort. However, when this love helps the beloved become independent, its positive side appears.

A person shaped by deep love grows more open and sensitive to others, increasing their ability to love more people. These new loves do not weaken the original one; instead, they strengthen it, creating a positive cycle. The perceived distractions of new loves appear to reinforce the commitment to the beloved. All of these dynamics occur solely within the framework of disciplined freedom.

Herbert Spencer, the philosopher, states, "In total dependence, he or she cannot freely give the self to the beloved." Moderate realism posits that a lover must embody both independence and dependence to freely offer oneself to the beloved and, in turn, to accept the beloved's gift of self without reservation. However, under the guise of arrogant independence, there often lies uncertainty and vulnerability. With appropriate emotional support and well-defined boundaries, this can indeed be a time of discovery, growth, and healthy interdependence (where one realizes that living entirely on one's own is not feasible, and others become significant).

In Old English, the term *freon* is associated with love and means "the free ones," from which the word *friend* is derived. Thus, fundamentally, love is liberating rather than possessing. Love and friendship are liberating, as implied by the term Freon. Consequently, love and friendship should empower the beloved to become their best selves, guided by their own insights and aspirations. Love that restricts freedom is superficial and merely selfish. It is no better than arrogance. The one who allows their beloved to be free from personal possession offers the greatest gift to them. This is undeniably the hallmark of true love.

Criticism in Love

In an intimate relationship, love is often challenged by criticism and conflict. This phenomenon is prevalent in all relationships and is unavoidable. True love understands how to express disagreement without being disagreeable and offers constructive criticism. A frequent criticism that one may receive from a partner is the accusation of selfishness. The individual is criticized for appearing to prioritize their own needs, being perceived as insensitive or unaware of their partner's feelings, or being labeled as lazy or indifferent.

Furthermore, one's criticisms of their partner can reveal insights about themselves. Some of the recurring emotional critiques directed at a loved one may accurately reflect a neglected aspect of the critic's own identity, potentially aiding in the recognition of their own lost self. For a genuinely loving individual, criticism or confrontation is not easily undertaken. Such a person recognizes that this behavior can be seen as arrogance. "To confront one's beloved is to assume a position of moral or intellectual superiority over the loved one." However, for a love affair to thrive, constructive criticism is essential, as it should focus on fostering the growth of love rather than placing blame on the partner. It addresses the actions of the beloved rather than attacking the beloved themselves.

Disturbing Revelation in Love

At a certain stage in a romantic relationship, partners often realize that the very qualities they once found appealing in each other begin to irritate them, leading their minds to perceive these traits as threats to their relationship. For instance, a girl's cheerful and friendly nature may initially attract a boy and foster his affection for her. However, over time, this same characteristic may cause him to feel neglected or rejected, particularly when she interacts with other boys in a similar manner.

The underlying reason for this reaction could be that he viewed his beloved as someone who compensates for the fragmented aspects of his identity that were lost during childhood. Through their union, he felt a connection to these hidden parts of himself. Initially, this dynamic appeared to function well. Yet, as time progressed, the complementary traits of his beloved began to evoke confusion and stir up complex emotions. Consequently, she became less alluring to him, and he started to regard her traits as taboo.

This reaction may stem from his childhood experiences, where he was discouraged from engaging in jovial conversations with the opposite sex, leading to the repression of certain qualities within himself. As a result, he attempts to suppress his beloved in the same manner that his parents suppressed him. In an effort to safeguard his own existence, he seeks to diminish the reality of his beloved. As his discomfort with her complementary traits intensifies, her previously tolerated negative traits come into sharper focus. The shocking realization is that not only will his needs remain unmet, but his beloved is also likely to inflict wounds upon him similar to those he experienced in childhood. Thus, their love relationship reaches its conclusion.

Social Psychologist George Levinger (1983) provided explanations for the diminishing of love relationships. One significant factor is the unsettling realization (as previously mentioned) that the behavior of the beloved, once perceived as "Charming forgetfulness," is now regarded as "boorish indifference." Another contributing factor is the breakdown in communication, particularly in the act of listening to one another. A final factor involves the acceptance and encouragement of criticism directed at one's partner from individuals outside the relationship.

Loving Many with Complete Sincerity

How many individuals can one truly love with their entire heart? If a person dedicates their whole heart to their beloved, what remains to offer to another? Generally, individuals tend to love one person to their perceived fullest capacity while extending lesser affection to others. Therefore, as a matter of principle, they deliberately refrain from engaging in serious relationships with anyone else; however, it is indeed possible to love many wholeheartedly, as the heart in this context is not merely a physical organ or a tangible vessel. It is not emotional attraction toward qualities in another rather the openness to love. It embodies a profound yearning for unity in feelings and willful sentiments. This profound intensity of love can indeed reach out to many. The act of sharing love with numerous individuals does not diminish the love bestowed upon a single person. While there may be variations in expression, it neither opens nor closes the door of love.

Love as an Addiction

It is commonly understood that addiction occurs when an individual consumes sufficiently large and frequent amounts of specific substances. The roots of addiction reside within the individual rather than the substance itself. Psychologically, love can be likened to a form of drug addiction. Chein, Winick, and other analysts view drugs as a type of substitute (dependency) for human connections. In this context, addictive love is closely associated with these observations. This is because, in addictive love, one experiences a loss of the partner, leading to complete surrender and an obsessive longing for the lover.

In a monograph titled "Being in Love and Hypnosis," Freud asserts that when a person's self-love is redirected from their own ego to the beloved, the beloved increasingly occupies the entirety of the individual's self-love, resulting in the self-sacrifice of that person. The loved object (the beloved) effectively consumes the ego. Consequently, the lover's ego becomes "impoverished; it has surrendered itself to the object, substituting the object for its own most essential component" (similar to hypnotism). Much like drugs, love also monopolizes an individual's consciousness, and the addicted lover experiences feelings of inadequacy akin to those of a drug addict. Addictive love inherently encompasses jealousy and possessiveness, leading the addicted lover to disapprove of their beloved's interactions with new acquaintances. This competition for ties and interests makes the beloved less reliant on the addicted lover.

The Impact of Childhood Wounds on Love

Childhood wounds encompass not only sexual or physical abuse and the pain stemming from parental divorce, death, or alcoholism, but also the psychological and emotional harm inflicted on the child. While some may be fortunate enough to grow up in a safe and nurturing environment, they may still carry invisible scars, as from birth, they are complex, dependent beings with an unending cycle of needs.

Freud refers to this as being '*insatiable beings.*' Even the most dedicated parents cannot perfectly meet all the evolving needs of their children. In the womb, the child experiences a sense of oneness, and for several months after birth, it continues to lack distinction between itself and the external world. This phase is known as the '*autistic period.*' As adults, individuals often seek to regain this sense of wholeness and enter romantic relationships with the hope that their partner will magically restore this feeling of completeness. This expectation can inadvertently lead to difficulties in their intimate relationships.

Challenges in Loving the Wounded

Individuals who experienced trauma in their childhood often struggle to accept love. They retain feelings of rejection and unworthiness. Even when they do accept the love that is given to them, they require frequent affirmations of that love. This need for reassurance can become frustrating for their partner. They may perceive their efforts as futile, yet they remain attached to their beloved, as they quickly feel a sense of emptiness without that connection. It is essential for the beloved to attentively listen to their inner struggles in order to understand their true needs.

Healing The Wounds of Childhood Through Love

The individual who experienced trauma in childhood carries those emotional scars into their subsequent intimate relationships in adulthood. This person may exhibit heightened anxiety, depression, feelings of isolation, helplessness, worthlessness, and rejection.

Freud pioneered the concept of psychological healing, which has since been expanded upon by the behaviorist school. They assert that, "If one has a sufficiently intimate and secure relationship with another individual, they can reveal their wounds." Therefore, the beloved must offer recognition, acceptance, and appreciation, which significantly aids in helping the individual to unlearn their past experiences and replace them with healthier ones. If the beloved is honest, dependable, and sensitive enough to respond appropriately, then healing can occur.

Healing is not a simple process, as the wounded individual often anticipates abandonment, rejection, and pain, and may interpret even the slightest misstep from their beloved as a recurrence of their fears. There is also a risk for the wounded individual in revealing their scars, as being ignored or dismissed by a beloved who seeks only enjoyable interactions can magnify their wounds. However, when genuine healing occurs, one discovers for the first time in adulthood what was lacking during their childhood.

4
Reciprocity of Love

Love flourishes most deeply when it is mutual. Reciprocity is a fundamental principle of a healthy love relationship. It refers to the mutual exchange of affection, commitment, and emotional support between partners. Love that is reciprocated fosters balance, trust, and emotional security, ensuring that both individuals feel equally valued within the relationship. In a genuine love relationship, reciprocity ensures that giving and receiving are not one-sided, preventing emotional exhaustion and imbalance. This mutual exchange extends beyond romantic feelings to include empathy, support, communication, and shared responsibility. Each partner contributes to the relationship while also honouring the needs and boundaries of the other.

The Nature of Reciprocal Love

Love encompasses both giving and receiving. It necessitates a simultaneous exchange of offers and responses. Accepting a partner's love validates the beloved as a cherished and valued companion (Scores,1997). If the beloved fails to meet essential needs, the lover may fall out of love, as a lack of response can lead to the demise of affection. The more the beloved fulfills deep desires and needs, the stronger the temptation to love that person becomes.

This reciprocity in love presents a paradox: if love is inherently reciprocal, how can one selflessly give to another without expecting something in return? The answer lies in the notion that the greater the lover's trust, the more assured one can be of the beloved's meaningful response. Furthermore, it is stated that "the highest level of reciprocal fulfillment can only be achieved through a partial sacrifice of individual fulfillment." Excessive expectations from the beloved can lead to complications, necessitating the sacrifice of certain personal desires.

In reciprocity, the focus is not solely on the other-centeredness between the lover and the beloved, but also on the beloved's complete acceptance of the lover's total gift. Thus, a healthy self-love underlies the other-centered love shared between partners; otherwise, their relationship may swiftly fade. For instance, a girl in love must recognize that her self-gift is valuable and that she is deserving of her lover's trust; otherwise, her giving may lack confidence and become weakened. Similarly, a boy should be aware of the appealing qualities he possesses that make his beloved's self-gift worthwhile. If he fails to recognize this, his response to her self-gift may be filled with doubt and guilt.

Open Dialogue

Nothing facilitates the progression of love more effectively than communication, which is fundamental in establishing trust and affection. Freedom is essential in open dialogue. The quality of love can be assessed based on the discussions between partners after they have been in a committed relationship for several years.

Self-Disclosure

Genuine communication involves self-disclosure; when an individual reveals their thoughts and feelings, even if they are not appealing or favorable to others, by authentically presenting their entire self, they demonstrate profound love and attain the pinnacle of love. Schulz and Rogers (1975) stated, "One way of viewing love may be as intimate self-disclosure. There is a feeling of openness between lovers. Both feel the other likes them as they really are, so they can be more open, more honest and more intimate."

Psychologists believe that when one opens up to their beloved as an act of loving self-disclosure, the other party will likely reciprocate. The fundamental reasoning behind this reciprocity is, "You have trusted me, and I will trust you." When an individual shares their feelings and emotions with their beloved, they remain true to themselves and to the love relationship. The extent to which one reveals or expresses themselves to the other serves as a measure of their self-awareness and understanding. Furthermore, the degree to which one conceals themselves from their beloved can diminish the significance of her love. They may perpetually fear that she loves only the aspects of themselves that they have chosen to reveal; and if she were to discover the entirety of who they are, she might not love them. Love follows upon knowledge, and thus, she can only love him to the degree that he allows her to know him.

Sharing Secrets

Dr. Marcy Crasy, a psychologist, states, "The concept of sharing a secret fosters a connection between individuals. It strengthens a relationship." However, such open sharing of feelings can of course be risky. Therefore, one must possess a significant amount of courage for self-disclosure, as that secret may also be disclosed to others, and there exists the apprehension regarding whether the loved one will embrace the darker aspects of oneself.

Halfway-Discussions

Engaging in incomplete discussions is considerably more dangerous and damaging. An expert remarked, "Divorces arise from unfinished communications." Incomplete discussions yield only adverse consequences. They generate muddled emotions concerning the beloved and culminate in resentment, ultimately leading to the demise of love.

Understanding

Knowing the true and authentic self of another person is challenging in a romantic relationship unless there is a willingness to share one's inner thoughts and feelings. Individuals often fear rejection for who they truly are, leading them to present a false image of themselves. They conform to what they believe others will accept, concealing their flaws, mistakes, and imperfections. To truly know another person requires a deep understanding: Perhaps the most obvious desire and need of love is to understand and to be understood. One cannot love what he does not know, and the highest form of knowing is understanding. Self-disclosure is crucial for fostering understanding, which can prevent numerous issues and doubts. Furthermore, discussions should be thorough and honest, as even a minor deception from a partner can significantly impact the relationship, raising questions about the authenticity of their love.

Love and Silence

In the early stages of a romantic relationship, silence can be considered golden to some extent. It is often said, "Words foster friendship, while silence nurtures love." "Love is not born from what is articulated, but rather from what remains unspoken." Conversely, in a mature love, silence can be dangerous as it hinders the potential for further communication. This occurs when one partner perceives the other as unworthy of sharing, leading to a lack of contribution towards mutual understanding. Thus, silence signifies a deficiency in love, causing the other to feel devalued or uninformed. Phillis McGinley expressed this sentiment poignantly:

"Sticks and stones are hard on bones
Aimed with angry act,
Words can sting like anything,
But silence breaks the heart."

Some individuals stop communication by crying, while others may express their anger through alternative means, such as slamming doors and leaving the vicinity. These behaviors are more indicative of childishness than a mature approach to addressing problems or issues. Love can endure significant challenges more effectively when addressed openly than minor ones that smolder quietly within: silence can complicate life.

Listening

Listening facilitates an understanding of another's perspective, demonstrating one's concern for them. Dr. Foely states, "Listening may not alter the reality of anyone's suffering, but it can alleviate the burden." A genuine lover listens attentively and recalls the moments shared. This reassures the beloved of his affection and care, leading her to grow fonder of him. Indeed, a decline in communication and listening among lovers signifies the decline of love.

Acceptance and Affection

Lawrence Casles (1969) posits that love partially arises from human desires for acceptance and affirmation. Individuals tend to select partners whose choices align with their own, avoiding those who might undermine them in any manner. This inclination leads to a bond with such individuals, as they provide validation, which serves as the foundation for love. Furthermore, "to truly love individuals is to embrace them as they are, with their strengths and weaknesses, preferences and aversions; love that lacks authenticity futilely attempts to reshape and mold the other according to one's own desires and fantasies." Such love perceives the beloved as a masterpiece to be realized: loving is like constructing a novel. There is always the desire to "draw out", the loved one from the lover's imagination. This artistic activity upon the things of the heart leads finally to the poisoning and termination of love. Genuine and pure love does not fervently seek to alter others. It embraces individuals as they are, for love yearns for unconditional acceptance, and only such unconditional love can bring about transformation in the life of the recipient of that love.

Love is About Individuality

A true lover acknowledges the beloved as an individual with a distinct identity, rather than as an extension of oneself. He honors and supports this individuality and the beloved's unique character. Thus, he grants freedom and refrains from attempting to alter her to fit his desires. There is a saying, "If you love someone, set them free." Relationships that fail to appreciate this principle can become suffocating and will quickly end.

Expanded Self-Centeredness

In a deep and reciprocal love, partners grow more human, each becoming more lovable not just to one another but also to those beyond their relationship. If an individual loves solely one other person while being indifferent to the rest of humanity, that affection is not genuine love but rather a symbiotic bond or an enlarged egotism. Therefore, a person who truly loves their beloved will also be more lovable to others and will cultivate additional relationships.

5
Genuine Love

Falling in love is not merely an act of will or a conscious decision. It does not represent an extension of one's limits or boundaries; rather, it signifies a partial and temporary collapse of those limits. It is a part of the great and mysterious scheme of true love. Furthermore, it is often stated, "Real love does not stem from a feeling of love. On the contrary, real love frequently arises in situations where the feeling of love is absent, as we act lovingly even when we do not feel loving."

Real love originates from a free choice made by a rational being who dedicates himself to the service of the beloved. This form of love encompasses not only personal attachment but also respect, empathy, understanding, care, and a readiness to sacrifice something of oneself for the benefit of the beloved.

Erick Fromm emphasizes that true love necessitates a lover to think, "I desire the loved person to grow and develop for his own sake, and in his own manner, rather than for the purpose of serving me." In a loving relationship, one should pursue unity rather than happiness, as true love inherently brings happiness.

Viktor Frankl cautions that a sense of well-being and happiness can only enter human life as a by-product. There is a well-known saying, "Happiness is like a butterfly. The more you chase it, thc more it will elude you. However, if you redirect your focus to other things, it will come and gently rest upon your shoulder." To experience genuine happiness in love, an individual must desire unity, oneness, and sharing.

Love, in its essence, is pure; however, when it yearns for happiness, it leads to a passionate unity. If the lovers are merely united by the desire for happiness, it cannot be considered true love, as love represents the union of two lives rather than two joys. Love serves to liberate and purify both joy and pain. When love is directed towards the pursuit of happiness, any physical separation that occurs due to unavoidable circumstances may diminish their affection for one another. Conversely, in authentic love, physical separation does not alter the true bond of love; rather, the more they are apart, the more they are united.

Additionally, Bowman (1974) states, 'Real love is centered on the other person; it is focused on one individual only; it embodies a sense of security and trust; it is constant, resilient, and meaningful, encompassing both emotional and physical aspects.' 'Genuine love encompasses both spirit and body, allowing the whole person to experience a sense of completeness.' Therefore, in the physical presence of the beloved, the senses of sight, hearing, and touch indulge themselves. Even the beloved is not physically present she still is not absent. The spirit can fly to the other's presence.

Movement of Ecstasy

True love involves the expansion of one's boundaries, specifically the ego boundaries. When an individual extends these limits through love, he reaches out to the beloved, whose development he aspires to support. To achieve this, the beloved must first be cherished by him; in other words, he must feel attraction, investment, and commitment towards an entity that exists outside of himself, transcending the confines of self.

Psychiatrists refer to this process of attraction, investment, and commitment as '*cathexis,*' indicating that one 'cathects' the beloved object. (Cathecting is the mechanism through which an object gains significance for an individual). In this endeavor, one also psychologically assimilates a representation of that object into oneself, and over many years of love, he becomes identified with that object (the beloved), resulting in a profound sense of ecstasy.

In this state, one feels more loving and accepting of all, experiencing a sense of inner unity. This is a transformative experience that alters his entire being and is beyond verbal expression.

'This love may carry presuppositions (of a metaphysical, psychological, and physiological nature) that remain entirely unknown to him. His love itself constitutes his 'experience.' He is aware of it, experiencing it with the complete fullness and depth characteristic of genuine love. He 'knows' far more about it than he can articulate. It is even conceivable that the effort to convey to himself and others what he experiences and 'knows' may result in entirely inaccurate statements.' When feelings are straightforward, they are easily expressed (for instance, hunger is painful). However, in love, the complexity of emotions makes understanding more challenging and nearly impossible to articulate.

Maturity in Love

Mature love encompasses the readiness to recognize and honor the individuality of one another. According to Miller and Siegel (1972), mature love is characterized as an action rather than merely a passive feeling. The act of giving is prioritized over receiving. However, this act of giving is not perceived as a loss, but rather as a fulfilling experience. Love evolves into a blend of Eros, agape, and philos. Rollo May (1970) refers to this blend as '*authentic love.*'

Erich Fromm (1965) describes what he terms 'mature love' as a representation of healthy adult affection. He states, 'mature love is union under the condition of preserving one's integrity, one's individuality.' This allows lovers to exhibit an 'active concern for the life and growth of that which one loves.' Furthermore, it is asserted that 'self-awareness or knowing who you are is an absolute prerequisite for genuine mature love.' On one hand, maturity calls for *independence*, the capacity to make decisions and adhere to them, and to find reasonable happiness within oneself. On the other hand, maturity involves '*understanding*'—the ability to value others, respect their talents and ideas, and comprehend their limitations. Additionally, another aspect of maturity is altruism. However, these three qualities are not innate; thus, mature love does not occur spontaneously. It relies on practice, personal development, and the experience of being loved.

Fostering a Healthy Love

In addition to the aforementioned points, several other aspects are highlighted for fostering a healthy love relationship.

i. Prior to embarking on a romantic journey, one must discard preconceived notions regarding the type of partner they wish to encounter. In other words, superficial attributes such as hair color and profession should not cloud one's judgment. Even upon meeting the true partner of their dreams, they may not experience a sense of recognition, as dreams do not manifest in that manner.

ii. An individual who desires to love and be loved must cultivate charm, thoughtfulness, and tenderness. It is essential to avoid defensiveness in an attempt to prove oneself right while deeming the other wrong.

iii. If the primary objective is to be loved, one is likely to fall short of this aspiration. A person cannot be deemed worthy of love if their main aim in life is to passively receive affection. Such an individual often exhibits emptiness and dependency, stemming from inadequate love in their upbringing. They may perform acts for others, but these actions are primarily to secure their own care.

iv. Love is inherently outward-looking. Therefore, a lover should prioritize the well-being of their beloved over their own interests. A true lover does not diminish the beloved's sense of self; rather, they honor her humanity and freedom.

v. To positively influence the beloved, when she treats the lover with kindness, he should reciprocate that behavior promptly and appropriately.

vi. It is crucial to value and affirm the beloved's unconditional and unique worth. One must be willing to forgive and forget the beloved's shortcomings, as love does not keep the score of wrongs.

vii. Understanding the perspective of the other, even in disagreement, is vital. Love entails a willingness to sacrifice for the sake of gaining.

viii. Being in love involves both the intention and the promise of lifelong fidelity, expressed sincerely rather than hypocritically.

ix. Lovers must engage in the exchange of genuine affection, leading to a mutual sharing of their true selves.

x. A person who has experienced failure in their first love must move on, as the love they once cherished is a part of their past, not their present. They can hold onto their memories but should not allow them to inflict pain. It is unwise to use the concept of lost love as a benchmark, as such comparisons can hinder success in new relationships.

xi. Integrity is crucial in romantic relationships, and deceit must be avoided. Infidelity can lead to significant emotional distress for both parties involved.

xii. Partners should be prepared to confront the realities of their relationship and should not assume that problems will resolve themselves through neglect. Delaying action until issues escalate into crises may result in irreparable damage. A lasting relationship is founded on trust and open communication.

6
Falling Out of Love

Currently, the rate of failure in romantic relationships is notably high. Individuals who experience love often find themselves falling out of it as well. Erich Fromm states, "There is hardly any activity, any enterprise, which is started with such tremendous hopes and expectations, and yet which fails so regularly, as love." This phenomenon may stem from the differing interpretations of the term 'love' among partners. In other words, they might possess two distinct definitions of love, leading to divergent behaviors that result in misunderstandings and disappointments. Those who experience despair often become irritable and critical. They may resort to negative tactics in an attempt to compel their partner to exhibit greater affection. They might blame their partner with questions like, "Why don't you...?" or "Why do you always...?" This desperate endeavor aims to elicit warmth and responsiveness from their beloved.

This raises a pertinent question: instead of expressing a desire for more affection, attention, intimacy, or freedom, why do they believe that inflicting emotional pain will lead to more favorable behavior from their partner? The underlying reason is that, as a baby, one did not smile sweetly at their mother to receive care; rather, they opened their mouth and cried, prompting a quicker response from her. The success of this tactic became an "imprint," a component of their stored memory regarding how to elicit responses from the world: "When you are frustrated, provoke those around you. Be as unpleasant as possible until someone comes to your rescue."

If an individual who employs negative tactics to elicit greater affection from their beloved is asked to identify a specific action that could enhance the beloved's feelings of love, they will likely be at a loss for words. This is because, during their preverbal stage, their mother met all their needs without them having to express a single desire. Consequently, a mental imprint was formed, leading them to believe that others should intuitively understand and fulfill their needs without requiring any effort beyond crying. To prevent such issues, it is essential to recognize that the beloved is not a selfless mother; she has her own needs and expectations as well.

Moreover, falling out of love is not inherently negative. A person's feelings of love can evolve over time, especially if they are not receiving a satisfactory level of fulfillment from their beloved. In a romantic relationship, it is crucial to avoid indifference towards the beloved and to acknowledge and respect their feelings. The individual who distances themselves from the beloved due to her negligence should not feel guilty about falling out of love, as this response is both rational and healthy.

The Viennese artist Gustav Klimt stated, "Better an ending with pain than pain without end." Therefore, it is preferable to fall out of love rather than to engage in endless quarrels and struggles filled with misunderstandings, suspicions, and hurt feelings.

Love Can Cause Pain

Loving and being loved frequently hurts, because in love one opens himself up to the pain that love can bring. Individuals who love but feel insufficiently loved in return may experience frustration. Consequently, the yearning to connect deeply with a partner and share intimate thoughts and feelings can clash with the apprehension of being hurt or rejected by revealing too much of oneself. Furthermore, when someone has taken away a beloved partner, the individual feels pain accompanied by a complex mix of loss and anger.

A lover shows care and reveals their true self, making them vulnerable to emotional pain. When such pain arises, the person may respond with hostility and anger, and at times, even with hatred. However, hatred is not the opposite of love; rather, it is indifference. Indifference signifies the response of someone who is not in love. A single negative experience of betrayal can be sufficient to make a person cautious. Once hurt, they may be reluctant to open themselves up to the possibility of being hurt again.

Ending a Relationship Without Causing Pain

It is an irrational belief that falling in love with someone necessitates marriage (as if life cannot exist without that person). In critical situations, individuals can manage their romantic feelings and choose to fall out of love if they are determined to do so. There may be valid reasons for ending a relationship, but it is essential to do so without inflicting pain on others.

Individuals who prioritize their homes, future, and genuine happiness—both their own and that of their partners—can transform their romantic relationship into a friendship or even a sibling-like bond. This transformation stems from their genuine affection and empathetic concern for the other person, leading them to avoid completely extinguishing their romantic connection. Consequently, they redefine their relationship as friendship or sibling love, devoid of sexual expressions. However, they must navigate several steps to end the relationship without hurting the other person's feelings.

- The realization that this love under a cloud cannot continue in its present direction.
- The shared concern regarding the relationship, allowing each party to express their feelings about the situation.
- Both individuals should perceive each other as still being attractive, recognizing that it is merely the relationship that

has faltered. Failing to do so may lead to feelings of rejection, which can be more painful.

- They ought to refrain from enumerating each other's negative traits and placing blame on one another.
- Gradually instilling confidence in one another, ensuring that each person feels valued and available when needed.
- Finally redefining the relationship as one in which they can be permanently comfortable as good friends, as agreeable companion, without the fear of going back to the first place of attraction.
- Some individuals seek an immediate separation, which is far from simple; it can be detrimental and may lead to feelings of frustration that could culminate in suicidal thoughts. Others engage in sexual relations before their romantic relationship has officially ended, viewing it as a form of self-sacrifice. Neither of these approaches is beneficial.

The painful experience of a breakup for the individuals involved is influenced by the intimacy they shared, the duration of their relationship, and the activities they participated in together. Consequently, such individuals often struggle to enter into new romantic relationships and find themselves yearning for what they have lost (Simpson, 1987)

Healing a Broken Heart

Romantic relationships are tested by lack of communication, and by geographic distance. When these relationships do not endure, individuals experience the sorrow of separation and ending a relationship is a difficult process that can lead to both emotional and physical fatigue.

Dr. Ted Richardson, the Director of the Marquette University Counseling Centre, states that coping with a breakup is similar to grieving the loss of a loved one. Furthermore, Professor James

Lynch, a Clinical Professor of Psychology at the University of Maryland School of Medicine, notes that the loss of a partner adversely affects one's health. The solitude experienced by the individual can lead to elevated blood pressure, heart disease, and hypertension.

Mending a broken heart is a challenging endeavor. The following suggestions put forth by Teresa Carson may assist in the healing journey.

i. *Recognizing the loss:* Acknowledging the loss is essential for initiating the healing process, as it is challenging for an individual to accept that their love has ended. They often hold onto the hope that it will rekindle, waiting for a phone call or message that they know is unlikely to arrive. It is crucial to come to terms with the conclusion of the relationship.

ii. *Accepting one's emotions:* The breakup triggers a range of painful emotions - denial, judgment, depression, and anger. In this phase, one may feel certain that happiness is unattainable. However, it is important to recognize that these emotions are a normal part of the process and will eventually subside! Time serves as a potent remedy.

iii. *Accepting support:* It is vital not to withdraw into isolation. One should connect with friends and family who genuinely care, as this interaction helps to reaffirm self-worth and provides a fresh perspective on life.

iv. *Keeping oneself busy:* Engaging in activities such as music, drawing, and other hobbies is beneficial. Assisting others can also serve as a distraction from personal sorrow.

v. *Should not seek a new companion too soon:* If an individual has not fully processed their feelings from the breakup, rushing into a new relationship may set the stage for further heartbreak.

vi. *Taking care of oneself*: It is important to avoid addictive substances (such as alcohol and smoking) and to focus on maintaining physical well-being.

vii. *Evaluating one's loss:* One must keep in mind that the pain is not permanent and this sorrow is endurable. Over time, that individual will recall both the joyful moments and the difficult ones. As Alfred Lord Tennyson stated, "It is better to have loved and lost than never to have loved at all."

viii. *Overcoming the memories:* To move on from the beloved, one should delete the conversation history and shared photos that are taken together and dispose the exchanged gifts and letters. Avoiding the places which they have visited together may help to some extent. One has to begin a new diary and eliminate his favorite songs that may evoke sentimental feelings. When thoughts of the beloved arise, one should change the topic and engage in activities that person enjoys.

Boys and girls who emerge from the experience of a broken heart feel liberated and unrestrained. They reconnect with their families and take pleasure in activities at home that they have previously neglected.

Experiencing Love Once More After Moving On

Reentering the realm of romance can be challenging following a breakup. It often requires time to reach a state of mind where one can appreciate the healing process. Some individuals may rush into a new relationship to demonstrate their ability to attract a partner of the opposite sex. This behavior is often a response to the blow to their self-esteem caused by the previous rejection, which now craves reassurance and comfort. Unfortunately, such endeavors seldom yield positive results. Therefore, it is advisable to refrain from pursuing a new romantic relationship until one has completely healed from the previous one.

Conclusion

Human beings are fundamentally relational in nature - a reality long recognized in philosophical, literary, and psychological traditions. As John Donne's assertion that "No man is an island" suggests, individuals come into existence within relational contexts and continue to develop through interpersonal connections across the lifespan. Among these, love relationships play a central role in shaping emotional development, identity formation, and psychological well-being. This book has examined love and relationships not as idealized or purely emotional phenomena, but as complex psychological processes that are particularly relevant during youth and early adulthood.

From a psychological perspective, love cannot be reduced to a transient feeling or viewed as an automatic pathway to happiness. Rather, it is a dynamic and developmental process that evolves through emotional maturity, self-awareness, and intentional effort. For young individuals, the capacity to engage in healthy love relationships depends not only on emotional intensity but also on cognitive understanding and moral responsibility.

The findings and reflections presented in this work emphasize that healthy love originates in self-acceptance, is sustained through mutual respect and effective communication, and matures through responsibility, empathy, and commitment. When love is approached with psychological awareness, it functions as a resource for personal growth, emotional regulation, and interpersonal resilience rather than as a source of confusion or distress.

This book further highlighted the role of attraction as an initial component in the formation of romantic relationships. Attraction, however, is not an isolated or purely instinctive phenomenon; it is shaped by environmental factors, social contexts, and personal experiences. A supportive and healthy environment increases the likelihood of forming stable and meaningful relationships. Equally important is a clear and mature understanding of the nature of love before entering into a romantic commitment. Although defining love in absolute terms is challenging—since individual perceptions are shaped by personal experiences and desires—the effort to understand love remains valuable.

A key psychological foundation of adult love relationships lies in early parental bonding, particularly the experience of maternal care. The mentality to hate or love seems to begin in the conception itself. So, the relationship between the father and mother must be cordial one. Attachment patterns established during infancy and early childhood significantly influence later relational attitudes, including trust, intimacy, and emotional security. When a child grows up feeling wanted, valued, and loved, this foundation fosters healthy self-love and self-esteem, which in turn enables individuals to engage in friendships and later romantic relationships characterized by mutual respect, freedom, and emotional reciprocity.

During adolescence, relationships with the opposite sex and romantic involvement become prominent. Entering such relationships requires shedding unrealistic expectations and preconceived ideas about love and partners. Love should not be driven by the need to be loved alone, but by mutual openness and reciprocity without coercion or demand. Honest communication is essential for deep understanding, while jealousy and possessiveness undermine trust and threaten the freedom of the other. True love respects individuality and autonomy; possessive love, by contrast, often leads to conflict and eventual disintegration of the relationship.

The development and maintenance of healthy love relationships demand psychological virtues such as honesty, sacrifice, emotional sensitivity, and appreciation of the other's individuality. When relationship dissolution becomes unavoidable, it must be approached with emotional responsibility and ethical consideration to minimize psychological harm. Furthermore, the process of recovering from relational loss requires intentional emotional healing. Individuals who have experienced disrupted parental attachment or emotional trauma in childhood may exhibit avoidance of intimacy and heightened fear of relational pain. Addressing and healing these early psychological injuries is essential for the formation of stable and fulfilling love relationships in later life.

In summary, love can be understood as an integrative psychological construct encompassing emotional, cognitive, moral, and behavioural dimensions. It represents an inner orientation that must be expressed through consistent, respectful, and responsible actions. When love relationships function harmoniously, they contribute significantly to psychological well-being and life satisfaction; when they are poorly understood or managed, they may become sources of profound emotional sufferings.

The psychological insights presented in this book aim to help individuals cultivate mature, balanced, and life-enhancing relationships by addressing common misunderstandings and emotional obstacles. Through such understanding, love can be experienced not only as pleasure but as a transformative force across all levels of human life.

Bibliography

DICTIONARY

1. CHAPLIN,J.P.,*Dictionary of psycology,* NewYork, Delpublishing Co., Inc., 1968.

BOOKS

1. ARGYLE,M., *The Pschology of Interpersonal Behavior,* England, Penguin Books Ltd., 1967.
2. ARLITT,A.H., *Adolescent Psychology,* London, George Allen and Unwin Ltd, 1937.
3. BATA,R.M., *Love How You Recognize It* , Allachabad, Better Yourself Books, 1977.
4. BROWN,R., *Psychology,* New York, Harcourt Brace Jovenovich. INC., 1953.
5. CARTHAIGH,B.M., *That's what friends are,* Bombay, Better yourself Books, 1992.
6. COLEMAN,J.C., *Abnormal Psychology and Modern Life,* Bombay, D.B. Taraporevala Sons & Co. Pvt. Ltd.
7. D' AREY,M.C., S.J., *The Mind and Heart of Love,* London, Faber and Faber Limited.
8. DOMINIAN,J., *Human Relationship,* England, St. Paul Publications, 1989.
9. DOMINIAN,J., *The Capacity to Love,* Landon, Darton Longman and Todd, 1985.
10. DRESCHER,J.M., *Now is the Time to Love,* ST. Paul, Better Yourself Books, 1970.
11. DUVALL,E.M., *Love and the Facts of Life,* New York, association press, 1963.

12. ERNEST R. HULL,E.R., *Love-Courtship and Marriage*, ST. Louis, B. Herder Book Company, 1934.
13. FELDMAAN,R.S., *Development Across the Life Span*, New Jersey, Prentice Hall, 1997.
14. FELDMAN,R.S., *Essentials of Understanding Psychology*, New York, Mc Grow – Hill, INC 1994.
15. FRANK D. COX,F.D., *Human Intimacy*, New York, West Publishing Co., 1978.
16. FREUD,S., *Beyond the Pleasure Principle* (1920), London, Hogarth press, 1995.
17. GIBRAN,K., *The prophet*, New York, Alfred A.Knopf, 1955.
18. HARLOW,H.F., "*Love in Infant Monkeys*" in scientific American resource library (readings in psychology, vol-1), (June 1959).
19. HASSEL,D.J., S.J, *Searching the Limits of Love*, Chicago, Loyola UniversityP, 1985.
20. HAUCK,P., *How to Love and be loved*, India, Sudha Publications Pvt.Ltd., 1987.
21. HEEN, F.J., *The Power of Love*, New York, Maco Magazine Corporation, 1964
22. HENDIX,H., *Getting the Love you Want*, New York, Henry Holt and Company, Llc., 1988.
23. HILGARD,E.R., *Introduction to Psychology*, New York, Harcout Brace Jovanovich. INC.
24. JAN,M. and LOSONEY, L.J., *Sex and the Adolescent*, Notre dame (Indiana), Ave Maria Press, 1971.
25. JEWELL, L.N., *Psychology and Effective Behaviour*, St. Paul, West PublishingC, 1989.
26. JOHN ALLAN,J., *The Human Difference*, England, Lion Publishing plc., 1989.
27. JOHN J. EVOY,J.J.and O'KEEFE,M., S.S.N.D, *The Man and the Woman*, Allahabad, Better Yourself Books, 1968.

28. KALAT,J.K., *Introduction to Psychology,* Pacific Grove (USA), Wadsworth Thomson learning, 2002.
29. KENNEDY,E., *Sexual Counseling,* New York, The Continuum Book, 1977.
30. LANDIS,P.H., *Adolescence and Youth,* New York, Mc Graw-Hill Book Company, INC., 1952.
31. **LEANER,R.M., *Psychology,* New York Macmillan Publishing Company, 1986.**
32. LEDFORD, J.B., *Adult Psychology,* New York, Harper & Row. Pub, 1976.
33. LEWIS,C.S., *The Four Loves,* Landon, Geoffrey Bles, Ltd., 1960.
34. M.ABATA,R., *Unlocking the Doors of your Heart*, Bombay, Better Yourself Bookds 1900.
35. MAY,R., *Love and Will,* New York, Dell Publishing Co., INC, 1969.
36. MC GCIRE, W., and HULL, R.F.C *C.G. Jung Speaking,* Princeton, N.J. Princeton university press, 1977.
37. MORGAN,C.T.and KING,R.A., *Introduction to Psychology,* Singapore, Mc Graw- Hill Book Co., 1986.
38. PECT,M.S., *The Road Less Travelled,* Landon, Arrow Books Limited, 1990.
39. POWELL,J., *The Secret of Staying in Love,* Texas, Argus Communication, 1974.
40. ROBERT A.BARON, R.A. and DONN BYRNE,D., *Social Psychology,* New Delhi, Prentice - Hall of India Private Limited, 2001.
41. ROBINSON, S., *You've really got a Hold on Me,* California, California Jobete Music Company, Inc. 1962.
42. SANFORD, J.A., J.S., and LOUGH, G., *What Men are Like,* New York, Paulist press, 1988.

43. SCHNEIDER, D.J., *Introduction to Social Psychology*, Orlando, H.B. Jovanovich Publishers, 1988.
44. SIGMUND,F., *Being in Love and Hypnosis*, New York, Bentham Books, 1965.
45. SMEDES,L.B., *Love Within Limits*, Michigan (U.S.A), William B. Eerdmans Publishing Company, 1978.
46. STANTON PECLE,S. and BRODSKY,A., *Love and Addiction*, New York, The New American Library of Canada limited, 1976.
47. STOTT,L.H., *The Psychology of Human Development*, New Delhi, the Macmillan Cof India Limited, 1978.
48. SUENENS,L.J., *Love and Control*, London, Burns and Cates, 1961.
49. THIBON,G., *Love and Marriage*, London, Burns and Oates LTD, 1962.
50. TILLICH,P., *Love, Power and Justice*, New York, Oxford University Press, 1954.
51. VANDER ZARDEN, J.W., *Social Psychology*, New York, Random House, 1977.
52. WATSON,R.I., *Psychology of the child and the Adolescence*, New York, Macmilliam publishers.

MAGAZINES

1. BAUER,G., *"A Parent's Guide to Teens and Sex"* in reader's digest, (December 2001)78.
2. CARSON,T.M *"Healing a Broken Heart"* in The Teenager, (February 1999)12-14.
3. DIAS,C.I., *"Friends Are Forever"* in the Teenager (November 2001)13-14.
4. FERNANDES,M., *"Friendship: what it is, what it is not"* in the Teenager, (February 1997)10-11.
5. GILLMORE,M., *"Where Loveliness Begins"* in the teenager,(January 2003)10-12

6. HALES,D., *"What friends are for"* in Reader's Digest, (March 1998)29- 30.
7. LAHEVALA,B.M., *"Immatured love/matured love"* in woman's era, 2 (july1993)33.
8. LORETTA,S., *"Friendship" in the Teenage,* (February 1989) 11-12.
9. PATRICK D. SOUZA,P.D., *"When the Flower of love Blooms"* in the Teenager, (July 1999) 18.
10. PUNNATHANAM,B., *"Fallin in and out of Love"* in the Teenager, (December 1997) 23-24.
11. PUNNATHANAM,B., *"Friendship: Favoured with love, wrapped in understanding"* in the Teenager (February 1998) 10-13.
12. REGO,N., *"Friendship in changing Times"* in the Teenager (December 1998) 10-12.
13. SANGMA,T.T., *"The little price – A story of friendship"* in Kristu Jyoti 20 (January 2004) 64-69.
14. SINGH,K., *"The Fine art of gift giving"* in Reader's Digest, (Feburary 2001) 124.
15. THOMPSON, K.,*" What Men Really want: A New age interview with Robert Bly"* New age, (May 1982) 30ff.
16. WILLIAM JAMES,W., *"Marks of Genuine Love"* in the Teenager,(February 2003)15- 17.